REAL & WILD YOU

your daring and magical inner journey

a self-coaching guide

REAL & WILD YOU

your daring and magical inner journey

a self-coaching guide

Inspired by the book: *Open Me — the true story of a magical journey from fear to freedom*

LEANNE BABCOCK

FIVE FEATHER PUBLISHING

Book production:
DIYPublishing.co.nz

©Leanne Babcock 2019
Five Feather Publishing

ISBN 978-1-9990350-0-6

For you who are ready to face your inner dragons,
discover true freedom and be the courageous, authentic
and fiercely compassionate being you were born to be.

Reviews for Real & Wild You

Real & Wild You is an inspiring and engaging read. Leanne has a gift to use her own life experiences to clearly convey profound truths about the challenges, depth and joy of this life. At times funny and at times deeply touching, this book is a creative, helpful and practical guide to enhancing our capacity to feel, to heal, be more self-aware and self-loving.

Karl Baker, Founder Mindfulness Works

Real & Wild You is beautifully written. What Leanne offers us in her second book is a powerfully honest, yet equally gentle examination of self—the lies we tell ourselves and the example of Leanne's strength to question the why of it all—that compels us to step into the courage to DO something about it! Real & Wild You challenges us to look ourselves in the eye and delivers practical, useful, easy-to-implement exercises to get at the core of ourselves and bring compassion to what we find there!

Darlene Stewart, Executive Director, Groups and Events, Cineplex

Leanne has followed up her first book *Open Me* with this deep, insightful guide into how we can truly find ourselves and our own path to a juicy, free, wild life. Over time, life happens to us, and we regularly need to be reminded to take stock, and to invite ourselves to go deeper into ourselves. How do we live a life of purpose if we are not free within ourselves? This book is for anyone whose inner voice is asking "is this it?", or "why am I not feeling fulfilled yet?" It answers so many other questions along the way. It is inspiring and insightful and I am glad she wrote it.

Melissa Clark-Reynolds, Office of the New Zealand Order of Merit

There is no doubt in my mind that *Real & Wild You: your daring and magical inner journey* is a handbook to help us live a much more courageous life! Leanne Babcock inspires us to go on a journey towards an intuitive, self-loving and self-compassionate existence and she does this magnificently through powerful storytelling. She also takes us gently by the hand as we saunter deeply into sometimes uncomfortable exercises that permeate our very soul at its core. This compelling self-coaching guide gives us the very tools to step into our profound truth and all the while fosters a hunger within to look deeply at our essence with courage.

Victoria Lorient-Faibish MEd, RP, CCC, BCPP, RPE, Registered Psychotherapist, Author, Keynote Speaker

Just simply reading Leanne's book puts you into a mildly meditative state, ready to open your heart. When you couple this with the exercises, it makes for a very powerful experience.

Kim Chamberlain, Author, award winning speaker, founder of Chrysalis for Women

Real & Wild You is a masterfully crafted hand-guide, woven with true heartfelt experiences and practical wisdom. It brings a fresh view and a wondrous way to impact our lives and our happiness. Leanne beckons us to go boldly into working on our inner journey, empowering us to greatness, with simple and meaningful ways for making changes to become more of our authentic best self.

Stephanie Phelps, Intuitive Spiritual Guide, Healer, Teacher, Ceremonialist — White Horse Journeys

The greatest and often most difficult journey we embark on, is the journey inward and moving from our heads to our hearts. Though it can be a pain-filled and humbling process, it brings with it the ability to see what we couldn't see, hear what we were unable to hear, accept without judgement or justification, love self and others unconditionally and most of all, understand the tug within that says there is something more. Even if you have done much personal growth work and healing, Leanne's experiences and exercises will take you deeper into your journey.

Paula Anstett, Author, Regional Vice President Arbonne, Vice President Kitchener / Waterloo Business Women's Association

Real & Wild You is an easy, entertaining read. Leanne provides information for further investigation into oneself. I found the book answered the questions my soul was asking, but that my mind hadn't thought to ask. Thank you Leanne for providing a great resource to use over and over again.

Annette Parker RRPr, Owner of ASP Coaching & Holistic Services

Leanne Babcock is the guru of helping you dive into your innate wisdom to grow, be more mindful, and shift from inside out. Leanne's stories and exercises in *Real & Wild You* are simple yet profound. An easy read where you can open to any page and find help.

Kaya Singer, Artist, Business mentor, Author of Wiser and Wilder, A Soulful Path for Visionary Women Entrepreneurs

Leanne Babcock skillfully and insightfully carries us, the readers, through the extraordinary journey of transforming our limits and fear in order to become our true and authentic self. The lessons, as well as the exercises are a powerful map to wake us up and unearth the deep wisdom within. As you read Real & Wild You let yourself be guided on this remarkable and courageous life voyage of discovering and becoming the "new" and integrated YOU!

Medea Bavarella Chechik, Feminine Power Coach, Transformative Therapist, Best Selling Author of Facing Grief With Eyes Wide Open

Disclaimer

This book is designed to be a self-coaching guide. It is not meant to replace the work of a therapist or a coach or to address deep emotional wounds. If in practicing any of these exercises deeper issues arise, it would be wise to seek assistance from a professional.

All of the exercises offered in these pages are suggestions. You are fully responsible for any actions you take as a result of working with this book. These exercises are not meant to cause any harm to self or others.

The inner workings of this self-coaching guide

INTRODUCING REAL & WILD YOU   **15**

i   Inspired by the book: *Open Me – the true story of a magical journey from fear to freedom*   17

ii   Real & Wild You self-coaching   19

iii   Why I wrote this book   22

iv   How to use this self-coaching guide   23

PART 1: LISTEN   **25**

Lesson 1 – Be honest with yourself   27

Lesson 2 – Receive an intuitive message   36

Lesson 3 – Distinguish your mind from your intuition   46

Lesson 4 – Leap and trust   54

Lesson 5 – Ask for and receive help   61

Lesson 6 – Do the work: take responsibility and heal emotional wounds   67

PART 2: TRUST   **77**

Lesson 7 –   Be with: this *is* the journey   79

Lesson 8 –   Open yourself and use your gifts   87

Lesson 9 –   Communicate with nature   96

Lesson 10 – Work with body wisdom   102

Lesson 11 – Trust yourself in challenge and fear   109

PART 3: BE FREE   **115**

Lesson 12 – Set yourself challenges to
          break through   117

Lesson 13 – Observe yourself and reflect deeply   123

Lesson 14 – Hold the vision and let go of the plan   133

Lesson 15 – Release all hopes, desires, dreams and
          expectations   142

Lesson 16 – Heal self-compromise and reclaim your
          power   148

Lesson 17 – Dare to love yourself   159

Epilogue   169

Acknowledgements   171

About the author   173

INTRODUCING
REAL & WILD YOU

INTRODUCING REAL & WILD YOU

i

Inspired by the book: *Open Me – the true story of a magical journey from fear to freedom*

Sometimes something really big happens that blows your world apart. In my case, it was something small. It started with a whisper, and that whisper triggered a thought from which I couldn't turn back—a thought that caused my seemingly perfect life to crumble.

Open Me – the true story of a magical journey from fear to freedom is the memoir I wrote about how I opened myself to the gentle voice of my heart—how I learned to listen, trust and be truly free. It is the story of a journey on which I faced my worst fears and was guided by my intuition and the wisdom of nature—the trees, stones and birds. Travelling to sacred places around the world, I deepened my exploration and experience of who I am. Magic and miracles began to happen as I found the courage to heal. Finally, I met the daring challenge of love with newfound freedom, and I fearlessly continued to follow the voice of my spirit to be truly me.

The lessons found in the *Real & Wild You* self-coaching guide are based on the journey described in *Open Me*.

Reading *Open Me* can give you some helpful contextual understanding of the lessons here, but it isn't necessary. This guide can be used on its own.

ii

Real & Wild You self-coaching

What does it mean to be real?

Many people feel something inside their spirits that they are longing to reach: a direction, a vision, a goal, a purpose. Sometimes they don't know what it is, but they can feel the desire for something to be different in their lives. Maybe something big. Maybe something small. Maybe they want to go deeper, fly higher, be bigger, be wilder.

After you are born, your personality begins to form and is guided by the culture, family and environment you grow up in. The development and reinforcement of your personality is based on your decisions and beliefs, such as: what you are capable of, how to relate with others, what is possible and not possible in your life. These conclusions you made are often arrived at unconsciously, but they are always made with the intention of ensuring that you are successful or that you are safe—in other words, that your needs are met and that you survive.

Many experts say that our basic personality is established before the age of seven[1]. This means these fundamental decisions were made by you when

---

1   **Brockway, L.S. (2014/8/28).** When Does Your Child's Personality Develop? Experts Weigh In. Retrieved from https://www.pgeveryday.com/family/activities/article/when-does-your-childs-personality-develop-experts-weigh-in

you were six years old and under. These decisions unconsciously guide your present moment choices. This is the reason why intelligent and successful people can end up making the same mistakes again and again, wondering how it is they ended up in the same position once more.

These decisions that guide your life can be unhelpful, firstly because they limit what is possible in your life, and secondly because they have been made by one so young without life experience and mature wisdom. I call these decisions "limiting thoughts." Examples of some limiting thoughts might be: I'm not good enough. I'm not wanted. I have to please people/be cautious/ be strong. I can't trust people. Good things don't come easily.

As you evolve in your life, parts of your personality can become constricting and limit the development of your potential. It can be like a box you live in or a shell that covers the real you. (Remember, your personality is made up of decisions. It isn't necessarily who you really are.) As you engage in the personal development work of dissolving limiting thoughts and beliefs, the shell starts to crack, the box begins to disintegrate, and your real self begins to shine through. You become more authentic, present, real and—wild.

Being "wild," as I am using the word in this book, is about intentionally cracking open the shell of old beliefs or stepping outside of the boxes we think we have to live in. Being wild is about listening to our own deep inner wisdom and connecting with our wider, natural environment, listening to the wisdom offered by nature. It takes being wild in all of its iterations—feral, extraordinary, daring and radical—to step outside of our own beliefs and unhelpful cultural and social mores that we have allowed to guide our lives.

As you follow the lessons in this book you may find that being wild is simply a more real way to be in the world.

Imagine being real and wild asking someone out, applying for a new job, initiating a project, starting a new business, speaking with that person in the elevator, apologising and healing a relationship.

That's inspiring!

Working with the lessons in this book is a daring and magical inner journey of opening you. This journey calls you to be vulnerable, to be self-reflective, to take responsibility where you haven't, to face your inner dragons. It's a daring journey that takes courage but when you take this path of opening to the Real & Wild You, it's a road that can lead to a fulfilling and satisfying life, and what I call—magic.

Are you ready?

iii

Why I wrote this book

After I published *Open Me – the true story of a magical journey from fear to freedom*, I had many comments from people saying that it uplifted and stirred something inside them. Some said it inspired them to take action in an area of their lives where they had previously been held back. Others said they wanted to take time to savour each and every lesson to absorb all of the learning. Others said they couldn't put it down until they finished it.

I realised each part of that book had valuable lessons that could be expanded upon in a way that could help readers absorb what was written in the story. That's what inspired me to write *Real & Wild You – your daring and magical inner journey*. This book dives deeper into the lessons of *Open Me* by offering complementary explanations, reflections and exercises, but it is also a stand-alone self-coaching guide and doesn't require the accompaniment of *Open Me*.

But the most important reason why I wrote this guide is that your own inner guidance always knows what is in your best interest. The lessons in this book help you to access and practice developing your connection with your own deep inner wisdom.

iv

How to use this self-coaching guide

This guide is intended for your own personal use, to support you in being your real and wild self through exercises that open you to your own deep inner wisdom, expand your consciousness and develop your intuition.

The flow of the self-coaching guide takes you on an opening consciousness journey: Part 1—to listen deeply; Part 2—to trust; Part 3—to do the work to free yourself. The topic of each lesson is explored through narratives, examples and stories, and each section ends with an exercise.

You can use this self-coaching guide starting from the beginning and working your way through to the end, or you can target specific lessons you want to explore. You can also use it like an oracle book. To do this, hold in your mind a question or an issue you are dealing with and hold the book in your hands. Then close your eyes and pay attention to the feeling in your fingers, any images you see in your mind or an inner gut-knowing as you flip through the pages. Stop on the page where you feel the strongest attraction and read that lesson as the answer to your question.

You might find that some of these lessons reveal more than you expected and that additional self-development or coaching are needed to open yourself fully to the learning and assimilate it.

For further assistance with coaching or for developing your own coaching skills, check out my website for coaching packages: www.leannebabcock.ca.

Thank you for your brave spirit in being interested in your personal development and thank you for taking the time and making the effort to use this book. I look forward to meeting you on these pages.

Leanne

PART 1: LISTEN

PART 1: LISTEN

Lesson 1 – Be honest with yourself

What does it mean to be honest with yourself? And what might get in the way of fulfilling this lesson?

If someone were to ask you, "Are you honest with yourself?" what would you say? Would you say, "Of course I am!" or would you hesitate?

A week after I had separated from my first husband, a friend asked me how I was doing. I knew she was asking out of genuine concern, but my upbringing told me I was supposed to have a positive attitude and be happy. That meant if I wasn't feeling happy, I had to lie about it.

"Good," I said, nodding my head and putting on a smile. I was actually scared, lonely and hurt, but I wasn't ready to admit that. Instead, I was "fine."

As you explore what it means to be honest with yourself, you may discover that you've never even thought about it.

What does this mean in the context of coaching? For me, it means being truthful with myself about how I'm feeling, whether it is pleasant or unpleasant, and being honest about what I really want. Not what my ego wants—what my soul wants.

Several years later, I was feeling unhappy in my

work and not sure why because I enjoyed what I did. I went into the woods and sat down on a bench to meditate. I thought maybe if I took the time to relax and listen deeply I might get some answers. As I was breathing slowly in my belly paying attention to the trees around me, a question arose in the quietness of my being: What do you want? At first the question didn't make sense to me. My logical mind answered back quickly, But I have everything I want. What more could I want?

Knowing that my thinking mind wasn't going to be helpful here, I closed my eyes and went deeper into meditation. It wasn't until I really listened that I heard a soft voice inside my heart say what I really wanted. The message I heard was: I want to live like this. This surprised me and at first I didn't know what it meant. Live like what? I wondered. But as I reflected further over the following weeks, the meaning unfolded. The message was about altering my lifestyle to live more in contact with nature.

I didn't know how this was going to make me happier at work but I continued to take action to follow that message, and it changed my life in exactly the way I was looking for and more.[2]

Being honest with yourself is about listening to your inner world—inside of you. This is what guides you on your path.

---

2   The whole story of what the message was and how it changed my life is in my book: Babcock, L. (2017) *Open Me – the true story of a magical journey from fear to freedom,* Five Feather Publishing, www.leannebabcock. ca/openme/ ISBN 978-0-473-39067-9

You might ask, *But what if there really isn't that much going on inside of me?*

I recall a time in my late teens when I was having a conversation with a boyfriend. Well actually he was doing all of the talking. "You're not saying much, Leanne," he said. "What are you thinking?" We had been dating for a couple of months, and we were talking about going our separate ways. I liked him, but I wasn't head-over-heels in love with him.

I looked down at the floor and shrugged. *I'm not thinking anything, really. What does he want me to say?* I felt embarrassed. I knew I should know what to say, but I couldn't think of anything.

"Well, how do you *feel* about things?" His voice sounded a bit more strained with frustration.

I kept my eyes down, this time focusing on my hands in my lap. I shrugged and shook my head. My lips stayed glued shut. *I don't know what I feel*, I thought. *I guess I don't feel anything.*

How could I be honest with myself about what was going on inside of me when I had no idea what I felt? Faced with this question, I had concluded that I didn't feel anything, but nothing could have been further from the truth.

There is constant neural activity happening in our brains,[3] whether we are awake or asleep. Our neurons communicate with each other mostly through the release

---

3   Wang, Xiao-Jing (2003/13/11). Persistent Neural Activity: Experiments and Theory. Retrieved from https://academic.oup.com/cercor/article/13/11/1123/274161

of chemicals called neurotransmitters.[4] These chemicals influence how we feel.[5] This constant activity is an indication of the perpetual flow of thoughts, feelings and reactions happening internally.

We are never not feeling something, and there is never nothing going on inside. However, we can become unconscious of our inner world and our feelings, and that's what had happened to me as I kept pushing my feelings down, ignoring and denying them.

There are many ways to push away or try to cover up feelings you don't want to have. You might eat food that you know isn't good for you. You might smoke. You might take mood- and mind-altering drinks or drugs. You might become obsessed with your appearance, keep busy, mind other people's business. These things become habits, and you might do them without even thinking.

It takes a lot of courage to pause and be honest with yourself—to stick your head in the well of your insides and face what is there. To listen deeply to the truth in your heart.

When I was in my 40s, my life was enviable in many ways. I was running a successful business, I was with a committed husband, we had a very comfortable lifestyle and we had just sold our house in the city and bought a property in the country. But something inside

4   Queensland Brain Institute, University of Queensland, Australia. Action potentials and synapses. Retrieved from https://qbi.uq.edu.au/brain-basics/brain/brain-physiology/action-potentials-and-synapses

5   Ehrlich, S. (2016/11/2). The power of thoughts: neurotransmitters and their effect. Retrieved from http://www.shdc.com.au/neurotransmitters/

me hadn't been feeling right for several months. I kept pushing the feeling aside, telling myself to stay focused on the changes my husband and I were making.

Even though by that time I had done a lot of work practicing being honest with myself, there were times when I got tangled up in the circumstances in my life, and it seemed like there was no time to stop and pay attention to how I was feeling.

Shortly after we moved into our new country home, I was carrying a box to our home office when I passed a mirror in the hall. My reflection caught my attention and I paused to look at my face. Looking into my own eyes, I saw a woman who was troubled. I shook my head and kept walking.

Was I going to listen to the inner voice that was communicating something to me? Was I going to pause long enough to listen to my heart and be honest with myself?

Another aspect of this is that being honest with yourself is not a constant state. It's not as though you arrive at the truth and then you're finished. It is an ongoing practice. Truth is not a static thing. We are evolving beings, which means that what is true in one moment may not be in another.

Let's say I am walking on the beach in my bare feet. My attention moves to the feeling of wet sand squishing between my toes, and I think about how difficult it will be to get my feet dry and clean enough to put my shoes back on. In that moment, I am feeling uncomfortable and not enjoying my experience. Instead, I am wishing I hadn't taken off my shoes.

Let's say I continue to walk on the beach in bare feet. I begin to think about all the toxins my body is releasing through the soles of my feet into the sand. I remember the documentary[6] I watched about how walking barefoot on the ground allows the electromagnetic energy from the earth to be absorbed into the body with healing effects.

As my feet feel the soft damp surface, my toes begin to wriggle and squeeze the wet sand. I'm having fun and enjoying this experience. I'm even thinking how I could come to the beach every day to do this.

In *The Shift*, a documentary movie about our shifting states of consciousness, Wayne Dyer explains a quote from Carl Jung. "What was great in the morning will be little at evening, and what in the morning was true will at evening have become a lie." What had been true for me one moment—not enjoying the sand wishing I hadn't taken off my shoes—was no longer true for me. My state of consciousness had changed.

You might wonder how you can tell when you are not being honest with yourself.

Over many years of practice, I have become more aware of when I'm being honest with myself and when I'm not. When I say something that isn't true for me, I feel it in the centre of my chest. It's as if there is a mechanism in the middle of my ribcage with cogs operating, and when the movement of the cogs feels disjointed in the moment of my speaking, I know something isn't right.

Another way to know if you are being honest with

---

6   Big Picture Ranch (2017) Documentary: Down to Earth. Retrieved from https://vimeo.com/205264910

yourself is to look in the mirror, into your own eyes, and to speak the words whose truth you want to test. Your eyes will tell you when you are telling the truth and when you are not.

Being honest with yourself is an ongoing practice and can be a challenging. It may be a wise choice to work with a professional coach or therapist who can powerfully listen and ask questions to help you discern your truth.

What are the benefits of practicing being honest with yourself?

The more honest I am with myself, the stronger and more resilient I feel.

The more I listen to the guidance of the truth of my inner world, the more fulfilled I feel.

Summary

- Being honest with yourself might not be easy if you have been brought up to believe that being strong or happy is good and feeling vulnerable or sad is bad.

- Feeling "nothing" is a sign that a lot is going on inside, but it's being suppressed.

- It takes a lot of courage to be honest with yourself.

- What is true for you at one point in your life will change as you continue to evolve your consciousness.

- The more honest you are with yourself, the stronger you will feel.

Exercise

Imagine the flow of your emotions as a river, constantly flowing and never the same. Where your emotions are not flowing, they become stuck and stagnant—just like a river. When you think you feel nothing, it is often an indicator that this is a stagnant patch of stuck emotion. This happens if you have been avoiding feeling certain emotions.

The purpose of this exercise is to help emotions to flow and to unstick any stagnant areas where you think you feel nothing. This will help you to expand your awareness of your inner world and to become more present in this moment. Over time, this exercise can facilitate a feeling of groundedness and aliveness.

STEPS

Create a way to periodically remind yourself throughout the day (from waking till you go to bed) to do the following steps:

Step #1 Pause what you are doing and take a deep breath.

Step #2 Ask yourself, "How am I feeling right now in this moment?"

Step #3 Stay with yourself until you answer the question with a feeling word. A feeling word will always be just one word, not an explanation. If you come up with an explanation of your thoughts or of the situation, ask yourself, "How does that make me feel?" Keep asking yourself this question until you come up with a feeling word.

Feeling words ARE NOT:

"I think…"

"I feel like he/she is..."

Feeling words ARE:

"I feel sad."

"I feel lonely."

"I feel angry."

"I feel content."

"I feel happy."

Step #4 In this moment of pause, notice the emotion inside you. Let yourself feel it without judgement.

Step #5 Do not analyse, overthink, try to fix or do something with your feeling. Simply let yourself have the feeling.

Step #6 Choose to continue with whatever you were doing or choose to do something else.

NOTE: As you do this exercise, you may find that old emotions begin to arise. This is good. Let them come so they can be set free. They will keep moving on, just like the river.

PART 1: LISTEN

Lesson 2 – Receive an intuitive message

What does it mean to receive an intuitive message?

Have you ever asked a question during meditation and received a response as a visual image in your mind or heard words or sentences in your head? Have you ever known something was going to happen before it happened? Have you ever walked up to two people and felt the tension between them even though you didn't hear them interact and nothing had been said to you?

These are all examples of receiving an intuitive message. Let's take it further.

Imagine that everything in the universe is energetically connected. I don't mean *pretend* that it is. It actually is. I remember seeing two photographic images of the sky shown in a documentary[7] by a scientist, Gregg Braden. In one image you can see a sky full of stars. The second image, which shows the same section of the sky, looks like cells and neurons in a human body connected in a web-like fashion. The second photograph is of the electromagnetic energy moving between everything and connecting it all. So

---

7   Braden, G. (January 2017) Deep Truths On Our Origin – Missing Links documentary series on Gaiatv S1:Ep3

everything actually is connected—by energy.

There are many ways to define intuition. For simplicity's sake, let's say intuition is the use of senses extended from and beyond the five physical senses to perceive the energy that connects everything. I imagine it as a spider on a web. Even though spiders have more than two eyes—and many of them have eight—most spiders, but not all, have very poor eyesight. Instead, they are highly attuned to vibrations, and they can pick up on the minutest touch on the furthest ends of their webs.

Like spiders, we are connected with everything around us by this energetic field, or web, of life. It is natural to pick up on the vibrations of energy around us. We sense it via our intuition channels: clear-hearing, clear-seeing, gut-knowing, and clear-feeling.

When I was in my early twenties I said to a friend, "I'm not psychic." I figured because I didn't receive graphic visual images back then, I didn't have "the gift." What I have come to realise, through my training and experience, is that everyone has intuition. It is natural and you are born with it. It is not a special gift that only certain people have. It is part of being human. As we expand our consciousness and grow, our intuition also advances and we can learn to develop it.

When I was in my teens I began taking courses to develop my intuition. I discovered that my intuition came to me often as feelings and as words I heard in my head. Sometimes it was hard to discern if it was my intuition. My logical mind wanted to understand and to find proof so that I could be certain.

The rational thinking mind often wants evidence and scientific research that justifies the truth of your intuition. But some things are just not meant to be understood by the mind. I liken this to times when I've tried to express something deep and powerful that I've experienced in meditative states and found that the words to communicate it did not exist.

I also believe that in some cases the science to understand these things also does not exist, at least not yet.

Developing intuition is a journey of bringing mindful attention to what your senses are picking up and trusting what you are sensing.

Here are some examples of our intuition channels:

CLEAR-HEARING INTUITION CHANNEL

When I was growing up, things sometimes got tense at home, and for a while I was really worried about my brother. At ten years old, he had already been in trouble with the authorities, and Dad was always extra hard on him, which made it worse.

I was scared, angry, and I felt helpless. One day there were so many emotions going on inside of me, it felt like I was going to explode. I needed to scream, cry, talk— but where does one go when one is twelve? The railway tracks came to mind. They weren't used that often, and they stretched out for miles over deserted land.

As I stepped over the sleepers, I shouted and cried, letting it all out with no one around. When the tears subsided, silence filled me along with the relief of having expressed my pain. The steady pace of my footing on the tracks brought a sense of peace to me.

"Why is my brother doing these things?" I asked out loud.

"Your brother is in pain," a voice said. I paused and lifted my head. I knew the voice wasn't a physical voice. It came from somewhere inside my head, but it surprised me. I looked around just in case. There was definitely no one else there. Up to that point in my ramblings I hadn't heard any responses to my questions and wasn't expecting any.

I kept walking and tested it out. Asking more questions, I received more answers—wise and helpful answers. A feeling of immense love and understanding began to fill me, and I knew that everything was going to be okay.

Clear-hearing is one of my intuition channels. That day on the tracks, I was receiving information from my own deep connection with the infinite wisdom of the web of energy that flows through all things. Walking on the evenly spaced railway sleepers was like an unintentional meditation that brought me into a calm space so I could hear.

CLEAR-SEEING INTUITION CHANNEL

When I am working with a client, I intentionally connect with the infinite wisdom of the energy of all that is. I begin breathing deeply and slowly and ask a question in my mind, *How can I help this person?* Usually when I do this I am shown a picture of what to do next in the coaching session to bring clarity, healing or a shift of perspective to the person I am working with. These images appear like a movie in my mind, and I simply follow what I see. Here I am using my clear-seeing intuition channel.

GUT-KNOWING INTUITION CHANNEL

Earlier in the year, as I toured with my first book, messages in my meditations guided me to stay in Toronto for the winter. My plan was to go back on tour in the spring so I needed a place to stay for only a few months. "I have a friend who lives in Toronto. Her boys have gone off to university and she has some spare rooms. She might be open to having a house-mate," a friend of mine said. I knew in that moment that was what was going to happen. No one had spoken with anyone yet, but I knew. I couldn't explain it. I didn't hear any voices. I wasn't shown any pictures. I just knew and I knew it immediately.

It was exactly what happened. This was my gut-knowing intuition channel at work.

CLEAR-FEELING INTUITION CHANNEL

A few years ago, I went on a ten-day silent meditation retreat where we meditated for approximately ten hours a day. One night, I woke up feeling very upset and afraid. It didn't make any sense to me. I had gone to sleep feeling good. Then I heard some noises from the room next door, where another woman was staying. I didn't know anything about her, because we weren't allowed to talk. As I listened to the sounds coming from her room, I realised the upset feelings I felt were hers and not mine. I sensed she was packing her bags to leave the retreat in the middle of the night.

The next day, she showed up for meditation and stayed for the rest of the retreat. I supposed I must have made up the story in my head. On the last day, we were allowed to speak with each other. I went to her and asked her about that night. She told me some personal issues had been triggered in her meditation that day, and she was so upset that she had decided to leave. In fact, she was packing her bags that night, but she changed her mind when she remembered the office of the retreat centre had her car keys and cell phone.

My clear-feeling intuition channel had picked up on her feelings. When we pick up on someone else's feelings, we may not realise at first that these feelings are not our own.

Often, one intuition channel is stronger than the others, but you can develop them all.

What might get in the way of receiving intuitive messages?

Intuition flows more easily when we are relaxed and calm. In the example I shared about walking on the railway tracks, as I continued walking after expressing my upset emotions, the regular pace of my footsteps helped me to became more relaxed and at peace. Then my intuition could flow.

By comparing your intuitive abilities with others or by thinking that only special people have "the gift" you discount your own unique intuitive abilities.

Always trying to logically understand the intuitive process can hinder it.

Having thoughts such as, "I'm just making this up," can get in the way and cause doubt. I'll cover this topic of doubt and the logical mind more fully in lesson 3.

What are the benefits of practicing receiving intuitive messages?

By developing my intuition I learn to trust myself. It builds my confidence.

I get to know myself by experiencing how my clear-hearing, clear-seeing, gut-knowing, and clear-feeling flows through me.

I access a wider source of information and wisdom, which can help me in my everyday life.

Summary:

- Everything in the universe is connected by electromagnetic energy.
- There are different intuition channels: clear-hearing, clear-seeing, gut-knowing and clear-feeling.
- Being intuitive is a natural part of being human. Everyone can access and develop their intuitive abilities.
- Comparing yourself with others shuts down intuition.
- Developing your intuition can build confidence and help you to know yourself more.

Exercise

Below are two exercises. As receiving intuitive messages requires you to be relaxed and calm, the first exercise is designed to help you do that.

Exercise 1 – CLEAR YOUR AURA

When you are developing and opening your intuition channels, it's important to begin by clearing your aura. As mentioned earlier in this lesson, energy flows through everything. The electromagnetic energy that flows from your body is your aura. This energy casts a light that some people can see. Other people can feel or sense auras. These are examples of people using different intuition channels.

Our thoughts and feelings influence our auras. Before practicing receiving an intuitive message, it's important to take the time to "clean" the energy flowing through you and to clear away unhelpful thoughts. Consider this to be like beginning an exercise and weight training program. If you did not support your practice by eating the right food and getting good rest, you would hinder your body's ability to assimilate the training.

We keep our physical bodies clean—why not the energy flowing through us?

It's best to practice this exercise daily, like brushing your teeth.

STEPS

Step #1   Begin to breathe slowly in and slowly out, deeply into your belly. Do this for several breaths.

Step #2   Imagine a bright light above your head (maybe a star or the sun).

Step #3   Imagine this light shining its rays down on you, and imagine these rays flowing through each part of your body down to your feet.

Step #4   Imagine these rays of light flowing beyond your feet and into the earth.

Step #5   Say in your mind three times, "Please cleanse and clear my whole being."

Step # 6   Say, "Thank you."

Exercise 2 – EXPAND AWARENESS OF YOUR INTUITION

This exercise is intended to bring more awareness to when and how your intuition works. In the beginning you might not notice much. Remember you are bringing attention to something you may not be used to paying attention to.

I recommend that you practice this exercise daily and write the results in a journal. It can be a nice way to debrief at the end of the day.

STEPS

Step #1   Sit down with a pen and paper and take time to reflect on these questions. Write down your answers:

- What intuitive messages did I receive today?

- Did I hear a word, sentence or phrase in my head at some point?

- Did I have any images appear in my mind during the day?

- Was there a moment when I just knew something—knew it was true or knew it would happen before it happened?

- Was there a time today when I had feelings that might not have been mine?

Step #2   After a week of observing your intuition, reflect and ask yourself, *What do I notice and what am I learning about my intuition?*

NOTE: If you are interested in developing your intuition further check online for my upcoming intuition development courses: www.leannebabcock.ca.

PART 1: LISTEN

Lesson 3 – Distinguish your mind from your intuition

What does it mean to distinguish your mind from your intuition?

When I run courses on developing intuition, I often hear the question, "How do I know I'm not making it up?" In my teens and early twenties, when I began developing my intuition, I remember having the same question. It is a reasonable question from your logical mind, which wants to understand and analyse, but it is not helpful.

Your mind, much like a computer, is filled with knowledge of what works and what doesn't—all based on your past experiences. It wants to keep you safe and avoid the risk of danger or mistakes.

But the question, "Am I making this up or not?" is unhelpful because it means you have to stop and analyse the intuitive process. In order to understand something, we usually compare it with what we already know and decide how it fits with that. Can you see how this could limit our understanding of anything beyond what we already know?

Trying to analyse the intuitive process also keeps your attention in your head, where the logical brain resides. But this is not where intuition takes place.

Close your eyes and bring your awareness to the skin on your cheek. Let your awareness rest there for a moment. You may begin to feel a sensation. This sensation is the energy flowing in your skin. This is part of your intuition—being able to sense or feel energy. (More about your intuition channels is covered in Lesson 2.)

Notice when you turn your attention to feeling the sensation on your cheek that the awareness of the sensation doesn't come from your thinking mind. Your mind may have commentary going on such as, "Am I supposed to be feeling something? What am I supposed to do?" or "I can feel something. What is this feeling? Am I making this up?"

From my experience, understanding my intuition from a logical perspective isn't necessary for it to work. The issue is more about trusting yourself.

Our intuitive senses are often subtle and quiet. Meditating and spending time in nature helps us to relax and slow down, paying more attention to our inner senses.

Not long ago, I was on a road trip across North America. One of the places where I stopped was Nelson, British Columbia, an artistic and alternative little town. I was arranging to leave a few copies of my book, *Open Me*, on consignment at the well-frequented shop, Otter Books, when a customer approached the sales counter balancing a pile of books she wanted to buy.

A voice in my head said, *Ask her if she wants to buy your book.*

I recognised this voice as my intuitive hearing. It is different from my own voice and doesn't come from my logical mind.

No, I responded in my mind. *I don't want to ask her that and impose myself. She is already buying six books.* I knew I wasn't making up hearing the voice. My logical mind had taken over telling myself I was afraid of upsetting people. My lips remained shut. The woman paid for her books and left the shop. I didn't trust enough in that moment to follow through with what the voice was telling me.

Ten seconds later, she walked back in. She had forgotten her keys on the counter.

Ask her if she wants to buy your book, that voice in my head persisted. Trust. Trust. Trust. I suspected that the universe sent her back in so I could speak with her. Finally I did. Within two minutes, she'd left the shop smiling with my book on top of her stack. As she left the shop she paused and said to me, "I've just moved here recently after going through some big changes in my life. I needed something like this." She patted my book and walked out.

And as if one miracle wasn't enough, here's what happened next.

The woman behind the counter—who had witnessed all of this—turned out to be the shop manager. She suggested that if I could speak to customers like that, I should do a book signing there. I wasn't staying in Nelson long enough to promote any events, so I hadn't initiated anything. Minutes later, I was in the calendar for a book signing in three days.

With no time to delay, in half an hour I had some posters printed. Then I realised I didn't have any tape to put them up. I wasn't prepared. Everything was happening so fast. *Where can I get some tape?* I held the thought in my mind.

I felt drawn to walk into a café on the other side of the street. As I approached the café, I started thinking, *This is silly. They won't have any tape.* Again, I didn't trust. I was afraid of looking stupid. I kept walking and didn't go in. I stopped a couple of doors down the street and looked back. Still feeling drawn to go into that café, I attempted to walk in again. But once more I doubted and kept going past its doors.

This time I paused and closed my eyes. I began breathing slowly and deeply. This always takes me into a meditative state. I felt the strong inclination to go into the café. I opened my eyes and walked in.

I briefly explained what I needed to the woman behind the bar, and without blinking she handed me a large roll of tape, as if she had it in her hand waiting for me—perfect for what I needed. "You can also put up some posters in our washrooms if you want," she said.

Trust.

What might hinder you from distinguishing your mind from your intuition?

Your intuition is often quiet and subtle. When you don't take the time to slow down, there can be too much noise in your head to be able to pay attention and listen to your intuition.

In busy moments, it's easy for the logical mind to take over and direct your life. Our logical mind does know a lot, and it has its place, but there is a deeper level of wisdom available to you if you tap into it and listen.

When you overthink things, it keeps your attention in your head and stops you from paying attention to your intuitive senses.

What are the benefits of distinguishing your mind from your intuition?

As I practice trusting my intuition and learn to distinguish my logical thinking from my intuition, my confidence grows.

I find myself paying more attention to the subtle flow of energy guiding me and move with it, like when I asked that woman if she wanted to buy my book.

When I listen and trust myself, I end up in the right place at the right time, and miracles can happen.

Summary

- *Am I making this up?* is a common but unhelpful question.

- The logical mind wants to operate from what it already knows and not take risks.

- Forcing something into logical reasoning can limit possibilities for growth and experience.

- Bringing awareness to your intuition often involves

paying attention to the quiet and the subtle, which usually doesn't come from the thinking mind.

- Meditating and spending time in nature can help to distinguish the logical thoughts from our intuition and make it easier to trust our intuitive senses.

- When we choose to trust our intuition over the logic of the mind, miracles can happen.

Exercise

The intention of this exercise is to help you to bring awareness to the difference between your logical mind and the flow of your intuition.

Remember, when doing intuition development work, always use the Clear Your Aura technique (from Lesson 2) before and during the exercise.

STEPS

Step #1   Choose a situation where you have a choice to make. Make sure it is something easy so you can pay more attention to following these steps. Examples might be:

- options for the route you travel to get home from work

- whether to go to an event with friends or stay home and spend time alone

Step #2   Do the Clear Your Aura exercise.

Step #3   Breathe deeply and slowly into and out of your belly for one minute.

Step #4   Hold a question in your mind that is related with the activity you chose. Ask the question using this wording: *Is it in my best interest and for the highest good…*

For example:

When I go home today, is it in my best interest and for the highest good to travel via the 401 Highway or County Road 28?

Is it in my best interest and for the highest good to go out with friends tonight, or spend time alone at home?

Step #5   As you hold your question in your mind, pay attention to your intuitive channels. Maybe you will have a stronger *feeling* for one option over the others. Maybe you will *see* a white light associated with one option more so than the others. Maybe you'll *hear* the answer in your head. Or maybe you'll just *know* the answer as soon as you've asked the question.

Step #6   You might notice if your logical mind has a preference which might be different from what your intuition is telling you. For example, you might *feel* an inclination to stay home and spend the evening on your own but you have thoughts like, *I don't want to miss out on being with my friends and I haven't seen Cathy in a long time…*

Step #7   It is always up to you whether or not you choose the path indicated by your intuition. If you choose the path your intuition has identified, notice if your logical mind has thoughts and opinions about your choice. They might sound like: *Why are you going that way? That's the long way. You need to get home in time to watch the news. You won't make it if you take that route.*

Notice that even though you can hear these thoughts in your mind, you don't have to interact with them or let yourself be guided by them.

Step #8 After a week of practicing these steps, write down your observations and insights.

PART 1: LISTEN

Lesson 4 – Leap and trust

What does it mean to leap and trust?

In the context of this self-coaching guide, the idea of "taking a leap" is used metaphorically to mean taking a step into an unknown space and without knowing what the outcome will be. Add trust to the equation, and it means taking this step into the unknown with an inner trust that everything will turn out okay, no matter what happens.

I remember when I was thinking of writing my first book. I had so many intuitive messages encouraging me to write, but my thoughts got in the way: *I don't know how to write. It's such a big project. I'm too busy. It wouldn't be good enough. There are already so many books like that.*

Then one day I was at the farmers' market investigating the gluten-free bakery stand and wondering which yummy morsel to buy myself. Another woman arrived at the stand. "What are you going to get?" I asked her. This opened up a lively conversation which we continued over a cup of coffee and some gluten-free baked goodies. I shared with her about my book idea and the story I wanted to write.

"You don't know who you're speaking to, do you?"

Barb said after listening to my story. It turned out that she was an American journalist traveling through New Zealand. One of the things she specialised in was social media and helping authors to launch their books.

"I'll help you with your book if you write it," she said.

I sat there blinking and looked down at the ground while her words bounced around in my head: *"If" I write it. Am I going to write it?* Thinking about writing a book and actually writing it were two different worlds.

I swallowed and closed my eyes. I was scared. In my head there was a whirlwind of thoughts: *What if it's a flop? What if I quit before it's done? What if it's just too hard? What if I spend all that time and money for nothing? What if I prove to me and everyone else that I really am a failure?*

I moved my awareness into my heart and began breathing slowly and deeply into the centre of my chest. My heartbeat was strong and steady. I asked my heart if it wanted to write the book. As I asked this question, my heart seemed to open more, and I felt excited. I sensed that my heart had been waiting for this. I looked up at the morning sun shining through the trees and said, "I will."

I had just taken a leap and trusted. I let go of trying to figure out in my head how it would work and trusted that the multitude of things I would need to attend to would be taken care of one way or another.

Here's what happened next.

Barb and I were sitting in a café discussing the title of the book. Somewhere in the conversation I said, "I'm just not confident with my writing." Having never gone beyond the desire to write a book, I had no idea what was involved. Within fifteen seconds, a man walked up to our table and said, "I'll help you if you want. My name is Phil, and I'm an editor."

It didn't matter whether Phil was the right fit for my work or not. At that moment, I was uplifted once again. This was a demonstration that the universe was working with me as I continued to leap and trust.

A couple of weeks later, in another café, Barb and I were discussing internet technology problems. She was creating a social media platform for me which involved adding a blog on my website. The new website software I had recently purchased was designed in New Zealand. Being a relatively new product on the market, none of the computer programmers she contacted had heard of it. Barb was very adept with software technologies but she was having trouble with the software I used. For the last couple of days, she had been trying to add the blog but it just wasn't working.

We were both frustrated. This issue was holding up our tight timeline. I put my head in my hands wishing I had never purchased this software. Who could we go to for help?

"Excuse me," the man at the table beside us leaned over. "I didn't mean to listen but I keep hearing you talk about this new software. I am a computer programmer and an expert with this software. I can help you."

Another sign. Leap. Trust. Trust. Leap.

Taking leaps and trusting like this doesn't mean blindly jumping into things and hoping that someone will catch you. When you leap, it's important that you have already checked in with your intuition so that you know you are making a good choice, like when I decided to write my book. When you trust, you assume that the universe is on your side, and you are in action and taking full responsibility for the outcomes.

What might stop you from taking leaps and trusting?

It's not as if my work was over once I'd decided to take a leap. There were times when it seemed too hard to stay on the task of writing the book. One night, I sat staring at the computer screen for two hours. In those one hundred and twenty minutes, I managed to write one sentence. I pushed the computer away. *I've had enough. I'm clearly not cut out for this. It's taking way too long.*

I got up and went outside for a walk, and during my walk other thoughts came to my mind. *You can't give up. You said you'd write this. This project means a lot to you. You can do it. Just write one more paragraph and call it a day.*

Once again inspired, I went home and wrote two more pages.

Unhelpful, doubting thoughts can prevent you from taking leaps. But just as thoughts can hinder, they can also help. When you start putting encouraging thoughts into your head instead, your whole inner world shifts, which alters your actions.

What are the benefits of taking leaps and trusting?

When I take leaps and trust, doors open.

As I keep taking leaps and trusting, particularly in situations when there is no evidence that success is guaranteed, miracles happen and my dreams are fulfilled.

Summary

- Taking a leap means stepping into an area of your life where the terrain is unknown and there is no guaranteed outcome.

- Trusting is about letting go of trying to figure things out, creating a sense of inner peace that everything will be okay regardless of what happens, and a willingness to take full responsibility for however things unfold.

- Checking in with your heart and asking if it wants to take this leap will help you to know if you are making a good choice for yourself.

- Doubting thoughts will stop you in your tracks if you let them.

- Encouraging thoughts are uplifting and bring you to a helpful inner state.

- Miracles can happen when you leap and trust.

Exercise

The purpose of this exercise is to bring awareness to your internal process as you prepare to take a leap.

To begin this exercise, identify something that you have wanted to do for some time but haven't tried before. Choose something small to start with, so that you can experience this process with some ease initially. To facilitate the language in the steps below, let's give a name to this thing that you haven't done before. Let's call it a "new action."

STEPS

Step #1   Bring the new action to mind and write down all of the unhelpful thoughts you have about it. Ask yourself questions such as, "Why haven't I done this yet?" "What is stopping me from doing it?" "What am I afraid of?"

Step #2   Answer this question: On a scale of one to ten, ten being highly important, how important is this new action for you? Note whether this answer is coming from your head (analysing) or your heart (feeling).

Step #3   Close your eyes and bring awareness to your heart centre. As you hold the thought of yourself doing the new action, notice the feelings that come into your heart.

Step #4   Choose to do the new action or choose not to do it. Do not let yourself stay on the fence about it. Notice the feelings you have once you have made your choice.

Step #5 If you choose to do the new action, reach out for any assistance that you believe will support you in the fulfilment of the new action. (More about asking for help in Lesson 5.)

PART 1: LISTEN

Lesson 5 – Ask for and receive help

What does it mean to ask for and receive help?

If you frequently require assistance with things such as household tasks, gardening, work projects, or personal care, it may be that you need to engage some kind of regular help—for example, hiring a gardener. Although this is within the realm of asking for help, it is not what I am referring to in this lesson.

A few years ago, I had a near-death experience. The river by my boyfriend's house had flooded, as it does every year, and he invited me to float with him down the river on inner tubes. I felt anxious about going down the rapids, but I didn't want to disappoint him, so I went. Not long after we started out, my boyfriend leading the way, I got caught in an eddy.

It wouldn't have taken him long to notice I was no longer behind him and he would have come back to rescue me. But that didn't occur to me. Instead, a self-reliant and independent thought guided me: *I could be stuck all day if I don't get myself out of here*, which seemed a reasonable thought at the time. I am a confident swimmer, but I was unfamiliar with rivers and rapids. I unthinkingly jumped out of my inner tube, hoping to kick myself back into the current.

There is a time and place for being independent and self-reliant, but being caught in a rapid is not one of them. This was simply an old habit for me and I didn't question being this way in any situation.

As soon as I got out of the inner tube, the swirling whirlpool of the eddy pulled me down like a flushing toilet. I got separated from my inner tube. The old life jacket I was wearing was loose enough to lift up and choke me, but too tightly knotted to come undone. I couldn't catch my breath. Struggling hard I managed to get out of the whirlpool. The strong current then pushed me into the raging river, and my life vest, now wrapped high around my neck, was strangling me.

"Feet first! Feet first!" Richard had gotten out of his tube and was shouting to me from the edge of the river. He threw me a rope but he was too late. I had already passed the point where the rope would reach and I was heading for a large rapid. A lonely thought echoed in my mind, *No one is there for me.*

I swivelled my body just in time and tumbled over the rocks before going under again, this time taking in water. My body was going limp without air. My head weakly bobbed up above the surface. I was unable to take a breath. The side of the river was a wall of slippery rock. In a last attempt to save myself my frozen fingers clawed futilely at the wet, steep rock. I remember thinking, *Is this it? Is this how I die?*

Then I had another thought. *I haven't asked for help yet.* Turning my attention to the greater consciousness of all things, I put out the thought, *Please help me.*

In that split second, two thin branches appeared out of the rock, and I grabbed them.

That was a life-changing experience for me.

Asking for help is about asking for and being open to receiving assistance in whatever form it appears, and not wishing that my boyfriend got out of his inner tube quicker, or the rope was longer, or the branches showed up earlier.

Ultimately, it is about being aware that there is a greater consciousness of all things. Asking it for assistance in times of need acknowledges a deep knowing that you are connected with everything and everyone.

What might stop you from asking for and receiving help?

During the episode I've just described, I ignored an opportunity for help. When I was initially stuck in the eddy, I could have stayed in the inner tube and waited for help. Sometimes staying where you are and allowing help to come to you is the wisest option.

Repeating old habits that stop you from reaching out to others can be unhelpful and even dangerous. It took nearly drowning to show me that I would have to change if I was going to keep opening myself to what is possible in life.

Old beliefs from the past can also hinder you. For example, *People aren't there for me,* or *If I ask for help it means I am weak.*

Wanting the assistance to show up in a particular way can also thwart your ability to receive help.

What are the benefits of asking for and receiving help?

Asking for help expands possibilities and can create miracles.

When I ask for help from the greater conscious of all things, I feel more connected with the world around me. I know I am not alone.

When I receive help from someone else, it can be a gift for us both.

Summary

- This lesson is not about situations where you regularly need help.
- Asking for help is about being open to receiving assistance in whatever form it appears.
- Asking for help from the greater consciousness of all things acknowledges a deep knowing that you are connected with everything and everyone.
- Old habits and beliefs can stop you from asking for help.
- Asking for help can create possibilities and miracles.

Exercise

In some cultures, particularly North American, it is praised to be independent, self-reliant, staunch and not require assistance. Many people hold back from asking for help and may not even think about it. The intention of this exercise is to bring awareness to the thoughts that can hold you back from asking for help.

You might choose to do this exercise for a week or two.

STEPS

Step #1 Put in place a reminder, maybe on your cell phone or a piece of paper, to sit quietly and reflect for five to ten minutes. Set the reminder for twice a day.

Step #2 As you sit quietly, reflect on a moment in your day when you could have asked for help but didn't. (Maybe in the beginning nothing comes to mind but persist with the exercise. It is about bringing awareness to something you may not be aware of.) Bring to mind the thoughts you had in that moment when you didn't ask for help. Notice the feelings that accompanied these thoughts.

Step #3 Write down those thoughts and feelings.

Step #4 After performing the above steps twice a day for one week, take time to reflect on your observations and answer these questions:

- What was the most common thought you had regarding asking for help?

- How did that thought hinder you?

- How does that thought impact other areas of your life?

- What did you observe during this whole exercise?

- Are there any new choices you might make after reflecting on this?

PART 1: LISTEN

Lesson 6 – Do the work: take responsibility and heal emotional wounds

What does it mean to take responsibility and heal emotional wounds?

When my marriage broke up, I experienced a lot of hurt. Sure it takes two, but he did hurtful things, I had a right to feel hurt, and it was his fault that I felt so hurt. Right?

Emotional wounding can happen in relationships when other people (parents, friends, spouses, siblings, bosses) do not fulfil our expectations or desires and we blame them. (I will cover more about having expectations and desires in Lesson 15.)

Of course I had every right to feel hurt. I have a right to feel whatever I feel. It is healthy to feel and to let those feelings flow.

But when I handle those feelings in unhealthy ways such as lashing out, blaming others or continuing to recount the story of what happened and how I was hurt, this causes a lot of wounding for me and those around me. On the other hand, it is also wounding to suppress and pretend not to feel what I feel.

So how can you feel and express your feelings in a healthy way?

Research has shown that our thoughts give rise to our feelings.[8] At a physiological level, electrical impulses in the brain both produce *and are produced by* our thoughts.[9] These electrical impulses release neurotransmitters, which are chemicals that influence how we feel. For example, a thought such as, *I'm not good enough*, triggers the release of chemicals that promote feelings of unworthiness.

Research also shows the link between our emotions and our physical health. When negative emotions are not expressed—or when they are expressed too often—this can adversely affect the health of our bodies.[10]

Taking responsibility in this context means bringing awareness to suppressed or over-expressed wounded feelings and taking helpful actions to enable a more resilient and healthy state—emotionally, mentally and physically.

My husband and I were still sharing the same house while we were going through our separation. I thought it would give us some time to talk and remain friends. I was trying so hard to be spiritual about the situation, telling myself that he was the one struggling and that I could handle what was happening without support.

---

8   Hampton, D. (2016/3/23) How your thoughts change your brain, cells and genes. Retrieved from https://www.huffingtonpost.com/debbie-hampton/how-your-thoughts-change-your-brain-cells-and-genes_b_9516176.html

9   Dougherty, E. (2011/4/26) What are thoughts made up? Retrieved from https://engineering.mit.edu/engage/ask-an-engineer/what-are-thoughts-made-of/

10   Psychologies (2011/8/24) The link between emotions and health. Retrieved from https://www.psychologies.co.uk/self/the-link-between-emotions-and-health.html

Really all I did was stuff down my emotions.

Three weeks into this, I woke up one morning to discover that I couldn't move. My back was so inflamed it had seized up.

By that stage, my husband and I were keeping as much distance between us as we could, so I didn't feel like I could ask him for help. Instead, I struggled on my own. I gripped the sides of the bed and wincingly dragged my body to the edge so that I could fall out on to the floor. Then I used a chair to manoeuvre my body to standing. Once I started to move, the pain lessened.

I already understood that my emotions affected my physical body, so this was no surprise to me. At a skeletal level, the spine and the back are the body's physical support structures, so it made sense to me that what was happening in my body represented the lack of emotional support I was experiencing in my life, but I didn't know what to do about it.

For weeks, I could barely walk. I knew that my circumstances and my thoughts about my circumstances were the source of my pain, but I was so caught up in what was happening that I felt powerless to change it.

Eventually, I went to speak with a counsellor. After listening to my story, he said, "I'm going to suggest that you write three letters." He didn't say the writing would fix my back. He didn't say it would do anything at all. He just gave me the assignment.

I could have decided that writing the letters was a waste of time or that it would take too much emotional effort, but I didn't. Instead, I thought, *what do I have to lose?* None of the letters were going to be sent to anyone. The letter writing was only a vehicle to help me to express the feelings I wasn't expressing.

The first letter was to my husband, and in it I said everything I wanted to say to him. It took a while, but once I found the core of anger inside, I let myself rage. I took the exercise further. I went into the kitchen, pretended he was standing there, and verbally let him have it. It felt so good. I felt the blood coming back into my face and an aliveness in my body that I hadn't felt in a while.

I was taking responsibility for how I felt rather than continuing to blame my husband and, by default, keeping myself in a position of victimhood. I claimed the anger that was underneath all the spirituality I tried to coat everything with, and by finding a safe and healthy way to express it, I could let it go.

In the second letter, I pretended to be my husband responding to the letter I had just written to him. I imagined myself being him with all the judgements I felt he had of me. I could even hear the emotionless tone of his voice as I wrote, "I'm sorry you feel that way." There was something satisfying about knowing what he would say and saying it on his behalf without him actually saying it.

In the third letter, I pretended to be my husband again, but in this letter I wrote everything I wanted him to say to me, including all of the acknowledgements and apologies I would never get.

When I had finished writing, I sobbed and sobbed,

my grief and my relief were so great.

The letter-writing process helped me to release the blame and anger and led me to compassion and forgiveness.

The next day when I woke up, all the pain in my back was gone. It never returned.

What might stop you from taking responsibility and healing emotional wounds?

When you continue to blame others or yourself, you not only cause more damage to your own wellbeing, but you also keep yourself in a disempowered victim state.

Healing emotional wounds often requires you to delve into some challenging emotions. If you listen to the sceptical, fear-based thoughts in your mind and allow them to talk you out of facing these emotions, the wound will remain unhealed.

Denying or ignoring that you have any wounded emotions to heal—as I initially did before going to the counsellor in the story above—can be spiritually, emotionally or even *literally* crippling.

NOTE: Healing old emotional wounds takes a lot of courage. It is very wise to travel this journey with the assistance of a trained professional.

What are the benefits of taking responsibility and healing emotional wounds?

When I cease to blame others and claim my own

emotions, finding a way to express them in a healthy way, I alter the neurotransmitters being released in my brain. This changes the chemicals in my body that may have been at the source of ill-health, allowing healing to happen naturally.

Healing old emotional pain also allows me to enter my next friendship or partnership with more freedom, less encumbered by old wounds.

Summary

- Emotional wounding can happen when others don't fulfil our expectations and we blame them.

- Our thoughts influence electrical impulses in our brains. These impulses release chemicals into our bodies and these chemicals give rise to our emotions.

- The over-expression or suppression of emotions can affect the health of our bodies.

- Taking responsibility means bringing awareness to suppressed or over-expressed wounded emotions and taking helpful actions to deal with the wounding; for example, seeing a counsellor, uncovering emotions underneath the surface and expressing those emotions in ways that cause no harm to yourself or others. This enables more emotional resilience and better health.

- If you allow sceptical thoughts to talk you out of facing your wounded emotions, the hurt and its impacts will remain unhealed.

- When you learn to claim your own emotions and find healthy ways to express them, you alter chemicals in your body that may have been at the source of ill-health, and healing happens naturally.

Exercise

This exercise is not intended to deal with deep, old emotional wounding.

The purpose of this exercise is to break the pattern of habitual and disempowering thoughts regarding a situation that has been troubling you. To do this, you will pick a situation where you have been blaming someone. On a scale from 1 – 10, with 10 being highly emotional and upsetting, choose a situation that is at the lower end of the scale, maybe a 4 or less. By choosing a situation that has a lower emotional threshold, your attention can be more on the steps of the exercise and your insights rather than on dealing with powerful emotions.

This exercise may take two hours or more and needs to be done all in one sitting, so make sure that you have sufficient uninterrupted time to do this.

NOTE: When doing emotional release work, I recommend that you find a trained professional coach, counsellor or therapist to support you.

STEPS

Step #1   Identify a situation where you are blaming someone or something. On a scale from 1–10, with 10 being highly emotional and upsetting, choose a situation that is at the lower end of the scale, maybe a 4 or less.

Step #2   Write down by hand (on paper, not a computer) the whole story of what happened, what or whom you are blaming and why, and the impacts this has had on your life. Include all of the details.

Step #3   Write the whole story again without copying what you wrote previously. This isn't a copying exercise. Let the story be freshly written. Make sure you write down all of the details of what happened, who you are blaming and why and how this has affected your life. You might find that new information arises.

Step #4   Write the whole story a third time including everything you can remember. As soon as you are finished, begin writing the story again. Continue writing like this until you notice something shift inside of you in how you relate to the story. You may end up writing the story ten times or more.

Step #5   When you have finished with the exercise, do not reread any of it. Burn all of the paper you wrote on.

Step #6   After burning it, take a moment. Sit down and close your eyes for a few minutes. Breathe deeply and slowly into your belly. Allow the healing to integrate without analysing it.

NOTE: Doing this exercise usually transforms the story you have been telling yourself about the situation and helps you to detach from it. After the exercise, the written pages have become the waste product of old thinking patterns and by rereading it, you run the risk of re-establishing those old patterns. Burning the pages not only physically transmutes them to ash but also symbolically releases and transforms the old patterns of thought.

PART 2: TRUST

PART 2: TRUST

Lesson 7 – Be with: this *is* the journey

What does it mean to be with: this *is* the journey?

To "be with" a circumstance means allowing it to simply *be* without trying or even wanting it to change. When I want a circumstance to be other than the way it is, I am resisting it, and this causes suffering.

For example, let's say I am on my way to the airport when I get stuck in traffic and miss my flight. If I resist this, I am going to get upset. Being upset on top of what I already have to deal with will cause me to suffer and make the situation more difficult to handle. If instead I choose to "be with" what has happened, then I begin to relax. This doesn't mean that I *want* to have missed my flight. It means that I am *present with and accepting* of the circumstances as they are.

As I relax, my mind has space to be creative and resourceful. I let go of catastrophising and thinking what I might have done differently and instead realise that I am exactly where I should be because this is where I am. This allows me to be present to my current situation and consider the opportunities before me. I can ask myself, *What actions are available to me now?* Upon reflection, I could reschedule the meeting I was heading to and research a new idea to present at the rescheduled meeting. Or I could take the rest of the day off and make it a personal care day.

"This *is* the journey" means that regardless of what I planned or wanted to happen, the reality of what *is* happening is part of a much bigger plan, and that *is* the journey I am meant to be on.

"Be with: this *is* the journey" means embracing what is happening instead of resisting it or wishing it to be some other way.

NOTE: This does not mean that you passively let things happen if you are in a situation where your safety is threatened. Immediate and appropriate action may be called for in such a circumstance.

A few years ago, I went on a shamanic vision quest and spent a night alone in the desert in Bear Wallow Canyon in Arizona. My intention was to remain awake and stay out in the open inside a medicine wheel that I would make with rocks and prayer ties.

Days beforehand, I meditated and visualised where I would settle for the night. Having never been to this desert canyon I didn't have any visual reference. In my mind I saw a large, smooth stone surface indented in the centre, almost like the open palm of a hand and the perfect size for me to lie in. The stone was a ledge that overlooked a valley. On one side of it there was a rock face, and on the other side was a thick forest of trees. It looked like a cosy spot to be.

My guide dropped me off at the canyon entrance just before sunset. I didn't have much time to find my spot and get myself sorted before it was dark and I wondered if I would be able to find the place I had visualised.

All of my senses were on full alert. My skin tingled as if every pore was on guard. I was acutely aware that I was in an unfamiliar place that was also home to coyotes, mountain lions and other wild creatures.

I closed my eyes and held the image of the place I had seen in my visualisations. Then in my mind's eye I scanned the path ahead and envisioned a path lit with white light branching off to the left.

I opened my eyes and began walking. Within a couple of minutes, a trail appeared to the left of the main path. I took it. Within five minutes, I had reached a ledge overlooking the valley. It was a smooth, indented stone with a rock face on one side and trees on the other. I had found the spot. My heart pounded with excitement, and tears filled my eyes. I had never expected to actually find the place in my visions, but I did.

Wrapped in my shawl, I sat inside my medicine wheel and watched as orange, red, pink, grey, blue and white streaked the sky. It was like being in the front row of my own private theatre, and I looked forward to watching every last ray of sun as dusk moved in.

But that didn't happen.

Instead, lightning flashed, thunder roared and the wind rose. Within two minutes, I was in the middle of a torrential storm. I had no umbrella and no rain jacket. My chosen spot had quickly become a large puddle. I eyed another place on higher ground, now more appealing, but remembered the words of my guide. "Stay inside your medicine wheel. This is where you have been sending your energy to," she'd said firmly.

My fingers futilely gripped the small piece of tarpaulin held over my head like a tent as the wind howled through it. I hugged my knees tightly into my chest, wondering how long I'd have to wait for the storm to pass. I was so disappointed that my shamanic journey had been spoiled by the weather.

As I sat there shivering, I had another thought. *How strange to think that I should be able to press the pause button on the parts of life I don't like.* I wondered how many other parts of my life I had on pause.

Something inside me began to wake up. *What a waste of time to wait and not live until things get better!* This *was* my shamanic journey, and I was missing it by waiting for something else to happen!

I decided that whatever was happening in each moment was an integral part of my journey.

I wrapped my flimsy tarpaulin tent around my body, mostly for warmth, lay down in the puddle, and exhaled a long, deep breath. The action I felt drawn to take was to surrender to the moment. My muscles relaxed as the water seeped into my clothes. Somehow the stone, the water, and the tarpaulin kept me warm. I felt held and soothed.

The storm raged for hours, energetically cleansing and clearing space for the new. Then it stopped, and everything was still. The crickets. The shooting stars. The expansiveness of the blackness. The night sounds. The day break. I saw and heard it all. My clothes had magically dried. I felt fantastic.

The storm *was* the journey.

What might stop you from being with: this *is* the journey?

When something is happening in your life and you think it shouldn't be that way, you are resisting what is happening rather than being with it. If you continue to think it shouldn't be that way, your attention and energy are focused on ignoring it, complaining about it or fighting it—all of which lead to suffering in one way or another.

What are the benefits of being with: this *is* the journey?

When I can be with what *is* happening around me, I no longer resist it. In the absence of resistance, I have more attention and energy available, which opens a space in my consciousness where I can be resourceful instead of suffering.

When I stop resisting a situation, it can often open up to become an unexpected gift.

I feel more alive and begin to trust that I have the resources and resilience to deal with whatever is happening in my life. As a result, new opportunities and possibilities can appear.

Summary

- Being with: this *is* the journey means embracing all that is happening in the present moment as if it was supposed to be happening.

- This does not mean being passive when your safety is threatened. Immediate and appropriate action may be called for.

- Thinking that circumstances should be different than they are causes resistance and suffering.

- Being with: this *is* the journey opens up the possibility for new opportunities and leaves you feeling stronger inside, bringing more vibrancy and resilience into your life.

Exercise

This exercise is divided into two parts. The intention of PART ONE is to practice bringing awareness to moments in the day when you react to situations with the attitude that they should be different than they are. You may need to practice PART ONE for a few days before moving on to the next part.

The intention of PART TWO is to begin to create a new habit of relating to circumstances in a more resourceful way.

NOTE: Do not skip PART ONE. When you focus your conscious attention on a specific habit, you will notice more details about your automatic behaviour. Being more conscious of an old habit makes it easier to break, creating more space for a new habit.

You may choose to do this exercise (PART ONE and PART TWO) over the course of one or two weeks.

PART ONE

Do these steps for a few days before moving on to PART TWO.

STEPS

Step #1   Make a daily reminder in your cell phone or on a handwritten note that says, "This *is* the journey." Read or say this out loud each time you are prompted by the reminder.

Step #2   Try to catch yourself in moments when something is happening and you think it shouldn't be happening or you think something else should be happening instead. Notice the thoughts you have and how you feel.

Step #3   Write down the thoughts and feelings you have when you are in those moments.

PART TWO

Step #4   Continue with your daily reminder message. During the day, bring awareness to moments when something happens that you don't like. Tell yourself, "This *is* the journey, and this is supposed to be happening." Take a few deep, slow breaths.

Step #5   Once you've let that message sink in, notice how you feel.

Step #6 Ask yourself, *Given the circumstances, is any action called for?* (Are there new opportunities arising? Is there something you have to say? Do you need to communicate boundaries? What action could you take that would make this moment more empowering, enjoyable or valuable? Or is the action to simply surrender and embrace the moment?)

Step #7 After a week of doing PART TWO, write down your insights from this exercise.

PART 2: TRUST

Lesson 8 – Open yourself and use your gifts

What does it mean to open yourself and use your gifts?

The word "open" here means to be open in your way of being: open in your heart, open in your mind, open to others and open regarding what you believe you are able to do.

"Your gifts" can be your talents and skills, your developing intuitive abilities as well as simple gifts such as a smile, a hug or a song.

A few years ago, I went on a tour of sacred sites in the U.K. It was late morning when we arrived at St. Augustine's Well, an ancient well whose waters are believed to have healing properties. Fifty of us spilled out of the two tour buses and walked down a well-trodden earth pathway to the Well. When we entered a lightly forested glen, our excited chatter hushed and stilled.

Rays of sunlight sparkled like crystals through the thick canopy of the tall old trees. Cool, fresh forest air tingled my skin. The only sound was the gentle patter of our shoes on the dirt. This was an enchanted place.

We gathered around the sacred well, still in silence. No one moved. We were spell bound. Then I heard the gentle humming of a woman's voice. I closed my eyes. It was beautiful. I wondered who it was. I felt an inclination to hum with her, but I held back. *You haven't sung in a long time. You'll be out of tune.* I stayed silent listening, but the desire to join in with her voice remained.

What will people think? They will all hear you. I tensed my neck. I still wanted to hum.

Was I going to be open and offer my gift?

The muscles in my throat relaxed slightly as a few notes escaped, softly so no one could hear. Then I thought, *I didn't come here to hold back.* Suddenly all my self-consciousness was swept aside, my throat opened and so did my heart. Sound began to flow from me as my humming danced with her humming. It wasn't any particular song. It was just humming and making harmonies. The music uplifted me.

At the perfect moment, our voices softened and silenced. I opened my eyes to find my new friend Angellica kneeling beside me, smiling. It was her. We had connected on the very first day of the tours and quickly became buddies.

Angellica took my arm. Tears filled my eyes as I felt the beauty and love of the shared experience. As we walked back up the earth path to the buses, Donna, another buddy from the tour, came running up to us. Her face was pink and swollen. She had been crying. "I just received the most beautiful healing from the angels!" she said. "They sang to me."

Angellica and I looked at each other. Our eyes widened.

Donna hadn't come to the well with the group. Instead, she wandered to another part of the ravine. She was too far away for the sound of our quiet humming to reach her through the thick trees—but she heard it.

I had opened myself and shared one of my gifts in that moment with no regard—once I got going—of how my gift might be accepted by others. What a gift that was to me as well as those who received it.

When being open everything else opens: your heart, your mind, your beliefs, your attitude and your world. Being open is a choice and has nothing to do with the person standing in front of you or the circumstances around you. Being open, most often, begins with opening your heart.

A year ago, I contracted my brother to do some editing work on my website. I really liked most of the work he did except one part, which I asked him to change. He disagreed with the design I had in mind. He attempted doing what I asked but it went against all of his design principles. We agreed to disagree and left it at that. I could finish the last piece of work myself.

I was part way through a 12-month road trip across North America and had paused in Florida. This gave me time to attend to some business things like my website. Soon I was back on the road, touring with my book, meeting new people, catching up with old friends and planning where to go next. Life was full. A month later, enjoying a cup of coffee in my camper, I thought of my brother and called him. No answer. A week later I called again. The call diverted to voicemail. More time went by. I texted him. No response. Time passed. I emailed. No reply.

Five months had gone by and I hadn't heard from my brother. It wasn't uncommon for him to not communicate often, but five months told me there was something wrong.

By this time I was in Nelson, B.C. sitting in the beautiful garden of a new friend. She was a fellow author and had invited me to stay with her as I passed through on my travels. It was Mother's Day and I had just finished calling mom. Holding my phone I watched the willowy flowers sway in the warm, gentle breeze. I knew there was one more call to make and I was having a conversation with myself about it.

Call your brother. The flower heads bobbed up and down.

I looked down at my feet. *No. I don't want to.* I was hurting and didn't want to be rejected again.

It probably has something to do with the work he did for you, you know. This had only just occurred to me.

Why doesn't he call me then? Why doesn't he say something? I wasn't ready yet to let it go.

I began breathing deeply in the centre of my chest and my heart opened. I was unwilling to keep holding a grudge. I dialled his number expecting no answer.

"Hey," he said gently.

Not prepared I said, "Happy Mother's Day!"

He laughed. "I'm glad you called."

My eyes welled with tears. The website project had

been the source of upset and he didn't know how to communicate it to me.

Sometimes the gift is a simple phone call.

What might stop you from opening yourself and using your gifts?

Holding a grudge will certainly hold you back.

Being critical of yourself or others will close your heart and hinder you from expressing your gifts.

Being concerned about what others might think can stop you from sharing your gifts.

It's possible that you're not aware of what your gifts are or you think you don't have any. Or you may think your gift needs to be really big to be worth sharing or that you need to be an expert before you can share it. When I was by the Well, it didn't occur to me that humming could be one of my gifts or that such a seemingly small gift could mean anything to anyone, but I was wrong.

What are the benefits of opening yourself and using your gifts?

When I open myself and use a gift, I feel uplifted and it can often uplift others.

Being open and sharing my gifts has allowed me to find my life's work and create my business through writing, coaching and the courses I offer. At the very least, it is an inspiring way to live.

When I am being open and using my gifts, people

are attracted to that. We uplift each other. Healing can happen. Unforeseen possibilities open up.

Summary

- Being open means opening your heart, your mind and your attitude.

- Using your gifts means offering or expressing your talents and skills, your developing intuitive gifts and your simple gifts (smiling, hugging).

- Being critical of yourself or others closes your heart and stops you from sharing your gifts.

- Gratitude and taking actions to contribute to others opens your heart.

- Being open and using your gifts is uplifting for yourself and others. It opens new opportunities.

Exercise

The intention of this exercise is to develop awareness of being open-hearted and closed-hearted and to create a practice of opening your heart with others.

The intention of PART ONE is to bring awareness to opening your heart with others. In the beginning you might not understand what it means "to open your heart." You may even wonder, *Is my heart open or closed?* and not be sure of the answer. This is good. It means you are beginning to bring more awareness to your heart. Keep doing the exercise.

PART ONE may take one to two weeks. When you have finished PART ONE, move on to PART TWO.

In PART TWO you will practice taking action to open your heart. Two practices that provide an access to opening your heart are: having gratitude and taking actions to contribute to others. Let yourself play with these practices as you experiment and bring awareness to opening your heart.

Once you start to practice opening your heart, it will become more natural for you to follow the inclinations you have to share your gifts with others.

PART ONE

STEPS

Step #1   Make a handwritten note or a daily reminder on your cell phone that says, "Open your heart." Read it every day.

Step #2   Throughout your day, bring awareness to moments when your heart is *not* open. (A few examples are when you feel: critical towards others or yourself, or righteous about something, or lonely, or driven, or impatient.) During these moments—when your heart is *not* open—notice what you are thinking and feeling.

Step #3   Write down those thoughts and feelings.

Step #4   After a few days of doing the above steps, take time to reflect on the thoughts and feelings you wrote down. What might be their possible source or root cause? Write down your reflections.

PART TWO

Step #5   Continue with your daily reminder. When you catch yourself in a moment where your heart is not open, experiment with these two practices and notice how it feels:

- Express gratitude for people and things around you. Here are some ideas:
  - Begin a gratitude journal and write down what you are grateful for.
  - Whisper to yourself, "I am grateful for…"
  - Tell someone, "I really appreciate the work you do, specifically…"

- Take actions to contribute to others. Following are some suggestions. Create your own actions that best fit your circumstances.
  - Give money to someone in need.
  - Notice someone needing help (for example, an elderly person being unstable on their feet) and offer assistance.
  - Take time to acknowledge and praise someone.

Step #6   As you do the practices in Step #5, notice how you feel.

Step #7   After doing these practices for a few days, take a moment to reflect and ask yourself these questions.

- What is my experience doing these practices?

- What are my observations about opening my heart and offering my gifts?

PART 2: TRUST

Lesson 9 – Communicate with nature

What does communicating with nature mean?

In the 1790s James Hutton, famous geologist, declared the earth to be a Superorganism that should be properly studied through physiology[11]. He was not the first to consider this before the 19th century. More recently in the 20th century, Lynn Margulis, a biologist and scientific researcher, and James Lovelock, scientist, supported Hutton's research discovering evidence that the earth is a living organism able to regulate itself, similar to the homeostasis of the physical body—self-regulating its temperature, healing processes, ongoing cleansing and renewal cycles—without human intervention.

Consider that every aspect of nature is a living organism and we are all inter-connected in the same eco-system. To "communicate with nature" means to exchange thoughts, feelings and ideas with other living organisms and beings.

A year ago I was working on an important project and had come to a point where I could not see the way forward. All the doors I wanted to open were shut. I was feeling stuck and frustrated, so I went out for a walk on one of the forest trails near where I lived. Being out in

11   Lovelock, J. (1988) The Earth as a Living Organism. Retrieved from https://www.ncbi.nlm.nih.gov/books/NBK219276/

nature always clears my mind and helps me to relax.

Seeing no sign of anyone else on the trails, I explained my situation out loud and asked for help. Just off the trail there was a bench facing some tall trees, and between the slim tree trucks were glimpses of the Grand River. I sat down on the bench.

A bird got my attention. It was a grey jay. As an animal totem, the jay symbolises vitality, assertiveness and going after what you desire. I watched as the bird landed on the lowest branch of the pine tree right in front of me. Then it hopped to the branch just above the one it was on. It lingered there for a second and then hopped to the branch above it.

I thought it was strange that the bird didn't fly higher or even fly to a different tree. Instead, it kept hopping to the branch just above the one it was on. It did this all the way to the top of the tree.

What odd behaviour, I thought. Then I remembered I had asked a question, "How do I get things unstuck when I can't see a way forward?"

I smiled as the answer occurred to me. I needed to do what the jay had done: stop trying to take big leaps in my project and instead take smaller steps, one at a time. As soon as I recognised this, ideas started to come to mind, and I saw my next actions. I had become unstuck.

We are part of an interwoven eco-system on this planet, and whether we want to be or not, we are in constant communication with each other via the electromagnetic energy which carries our thoughts and feelings out into the environment. You can learn to consciously work with this energy.

At the shamanic retreats I run, one of the exercises I teach is to be outside on your own and have a dialogue with nature beings: trees, rocks, water. When you do this exercise, it's helpful to have a question to work with in order to give the communication purpose and focus.

I believe that everyone has the ability to communicate with nature, and I do it often myself. A few years ago, there was an aspect of my life that was troubling me, so I decided to go to nature to ask for guidance.

Facing a purple flowered bush, I took a moment to be present with the bush. I looked at specific branches, noticed the size and shape of the leaves and the variable purple colours of the flowers. Then breathing slowly and deeply in my belly, I held this question in my mind: *How do I find peace?*

Nature communicates with us in various ways. One way is through physical demonstration, like the bird I saw that hopped from branch to branch. Another way nature communicates with us is through our intuitive channels: clear-seeing, clear-hearing, clear-feeling and gut-knowing. (In Lesson 2 we explore these intuitive channels and how they work.)

As one of my intuitive channels is clear-hearing, the response from the purple flowered bush came in the form of words in my mind.

The bush said, "What's peace?"

I pondered this question and reached down deep within myself to find an answer. When I responded, I took time with each word to make sure it was exactly what I meant. "Peace is when things are still," I said.

The branch said, "I don't know what peace is. I just grow."

Figuring that I had asked the wrong nature being, I walked on and found a small tree. I asked the tree my question, and its response was also, "What's peace?"

"Well," I said. "Peace…is when…things are…quiet."

"I don't understand what peace is," the small tree said. "The sun shines, and I grow. The rain rains, and I grow. The wind blows, and I move around, and I grow."

I was beginning to get my answer.

As I pondered the message from the tree and the bush, my body relaxed and my insight expanded. I was hoping for things around me to stop moving to give me peace, when really I needed to be at peace with the movement of my life.

As the message sunk in, the agitation I felt about my situation disappeared, and I was filled with a feeling of peace.

What might stop you from communicating with nature?

The first obstacle is simply not asking for help.

Once you do ask for help, sceptical thoughts such as, *This is just a coincidence or, I'm making this up* can stop you from listening to what nature is telling you.

When I saw the jay move up the tree one branch at

a time, I could have been sceptical and decided that it was just a coincidence. I could have told myself that birds can't give people guidance, and when I received guidance, I could have decided that I'd figured it out by myself. The logical mind thinks that it has to know and explain everything. This can limit or invalidate our access to and trust in a deeper wisdom.

What are the benefits of communicating with nature?

When I am consciously working with nature, I feel more alive and connected.

I have access to a wider spectrum of wisdom, and my consciousness is expanded.

More possibilities become available, and I feel uplifted.

Summary

- "Communicating with nature" is exchanging thoughts, feelings and ideas with other living organisms.

- You can send communication to nature telepathically by holding a question in your mind or by speaking out loud.

- You can receive communication from nature in various ways. One is physical demonstration (for example, a bird flying in a particular direction). Another is your intuitive channels (clear-hearing, clear-seeing, clear-feeling and gut-knowing).

- Not asking for help in the first place or having sceptical thoughts when you do ask for help can impede your communication with nature.

- Communicating with nature brings a sense of well-being and allows for expanded consciousness.

Exercise

The intention of this exercise is to get into the practice of receiving messages from nature. To begin or continue in this practice yourself, try the following:

STEPS

Step #1 For one week (or longer if you wish), each day when you step outside for the first time, hold this question in your mind and telepathically send it out to nature: *What is your message for me today?*

Step #2 Stay still for a few moments while you listen for the answer. Pay attention to what you see, feel or hear. Your answer will be the first thing that catches your attention.

Step #3 Once you receive the message (even though you may not understand the message yet), send gratitude to nature for the communication.

Step #4 Reflect for a few moments on the meaning of this message and how it might relate to your day. Sometimes the meaning of the message unfolds later in the day.

PART 2: TRUST

Lesson 10 – Work with body wisdom

What does work with body wisdom mean?

The body is made up of an estimated 37 trillion cells.12 Each of these cells has a memory, which is how they replicate—they pass on their memories. This means that the body has its own knowledge, aside from our intellectual knowledge, which I call "body wisdom."

A few years ago, I went to Arizona, a place I had wanted to visit for some time. I decided to explore some walking trails in the Sedona area. As I started off on this particular walk, I set two intentions. The first one was to remember who I was.

It wasn't that I couldn't remember my name or the details of my life. What I was hoping to remember was beyond what I consciously knew. I wanted my walk to be a spiritual experience where I opened myself to the world around me, paying deep attention to the subtleties of the moment and allowing myself to access wisdom I'd forgotten I had.

The second intention was to find a good walking stick for my excursion into one of the canyons. In my

12   Bianconi, E. and community (2013/7/5) An estimation of the number of cells in the human body. Annals of Human Biology Volume 40, 2013 Issue 6. Retrieved from https://www.tandfonline.com/doi/full/10.3109/03014460.2013.807878

meditations about this expedition in the canyon, I had seen myself walking with a stick, so I wanted to find one.

Three people returning from a walk approached me on the dirt path. "That's a really nice stick you have there," I said to one of the women. The piece of wood she was carrying was about five feet tall and looked like it was hand carved, although it wasn't.

She handed it to me. "Here, you can have it," she said. "I have to travel back home to Germany tomorrow and won't be able to take it with me."

My fingers wrapped around the unexpected gift. I thought I would find some old branch on the ground along the trail, but to receive this, and within minutes of setting the intention, left me feeling profoundly grateful. I held the stick to my chest and breathed in deeply. *Thank you.*

Setting intentions is very powerful. (More on setting intentions is covered in Lesson 15.)

But now I had a problem as I assessed the trail ahead of me. I was hiking up a rock mountain, and some of the trail would require me to climb using both hands and legs. I could carry the stick, but it would be cumbersome. I looked around for a place to hide my special piece of wood and decided to tuck it behind a twisted juniper tree that had fallen over near the marked path. I knew I would find it there on my way back.

Hands free once again, I carried on.

After my hike up the steep rock, I returned to reclaim my stick. I located the twisted juniper tree, but the stick was gone! I peered more closely at the fallen tree. Was it the same one? I looked around and saw another twisted juniper tree that had fallen by the path. *Ah, that's where it is*, I thought with relief. But it wasn't.

I scanned the area around me and noticed, for the first time, that there were *multiple* marked paths, and juniper trees were on the ground around all the trails. Fallen, twisted juniper trees were everywhere!

I looked behind a few of the fallen trees around me. Nothing. I scrutinised the area again and tried to recall which track I had taken. *Maybe it was that path. No I think it was this one. But it could have been the one over there.* I was feeling distressed. *Have I lost my special stick when I only just found it?*

I began to feel the heaviness of disappointment in my heart when it occurred to me: my head was trying to figure things out logically, and that wasn't working. But it wasn't my head that lay the stick down. My body knew where the stick was, because my body put it there!

I slowed down my breathing and began drawing my breath deeply into my belly. I brought to mind the image of my stick behind the fallen tree and telepathically I asked the question: *Where is it?* Then I relaxed my body and paid attention to where it felt inclined to move. As my body moved instinctively, my mind nagged: *I've already looked there. It isn't in that direction. I was never over there.*

Ignoring my thoughts, I kept following where my body wanted to go. From the outside, it must have looked like I was wandering aimlessly, but within a few minutes I found my stick.

Using body wisdom is an instinctual process—relying

on and listening to the cells of your body to guide you.

During my time in Sedona I decided to climb Bell Rock. It was one of the large red rocks 1,499 metres high resembling the shape of a bell. I had felt so drawn to go to the rock and in my excitement I climbed as high as I could, straying off the marked trail. Standing near the top of the rock on a ledge, my arms outstretched to the sun, I looked out to the vast horizon and breathed in the exhilaration of the moment.

After some meditation time, a breeze brushed my cheek. I opened my eyes and looked up. Clouds had moved in on what had been a clear blue sky. I could smell rain not far away. It was time to go. Retracing my steps I looked for the way down. *I'm sure I stepped this way.* All I could see was sheer drop from the ledge with no place to step down from.

After ten minutes of searching, finding no opportunity to descend, I paused. I could feel panic rising in my chest. No one knew I was here. I had gone a long way from the marked trail. No one would find me.

I began to breathe deeply and slowly in my belly. I felt the resoluteness in my body that I was going to find a way to get down, but how?

Then I had a thought, *My head didn't climb the rock. My body did. My body knows how to get down.* The situation was urgent. I spoke a command telepathically to my body, *Head, you are offline! Body, get me down!*

Without further thought, my body began to move in ways I didn't think it could. My arms. My legs. I felt like a wild cat—a black panther came to mind—negotiating the rocks and crevices of my descent. Within moments I was standing once more at the bottom of the rock.

What might stop you from working with body wisdom?

Rational thinking has its place, but when you use only logical thinking to assess a situation, you limit the pool of wisdom available to you, and you can't hear the communication of your body. This is especially true when you are under stress.

What are the benefits of working with body wisdom?

Asking my body for its wisdom can help me to resolve situations with less effort than I might expect.

I feel more connected with the natural world around me, which can be uplifting and healing.

Summary

- Every cell in your body has memory, which holds "body wisdom."

- Working with body wisdom gives you an expanded source of wisdom beyond what you can receive from your rational mind alone.

- You can access your body wisdom by breathing deeply into your belly and paying attention to where you feel inclined to move.

- Listening to thoughts that discount subtle communications from your body can interrupt your access to your body's wisdom.

- When you listen to your body, you may find that you feel more interconnected and uplifted.

Exercise

The intention of this exercise is to create some fun and to encourage you to play as you practice listening to your body.

STEPS

Step #1   Bring to mind something you have misplaced. You should be the last person who handled it, so wherever it is, your body put it there. Choose something that you are not worried about, as this can place added pressure on you to find it—now!

Step #2   Let go of the pressure of having to find it. If it helps, have a conversation with yourself about what you will need to do if you don't find it.

Step #3   Begin to breathe deeply and slowly into your belly. This helps you to relax and helps oxygenate the cells in your gut brain, awakening your instincts.

Step #4   Hold in your mind an image of the object you are looking for. At the same time, telepathically hold the question: *Where is it?*

Step #5   As you keep holding the image of the object in your mind, continue to breathe deeply and slowly into your belly. Lower your eyes to look at the ground to reduce the number of visual stimuli around you, and pay attention to the inner environment of your body. Notice where you feel inclined to move and move your body in that direction. You might also see images in your mind that give you clues about where to look. Let yourself follow them all. Have fun.

NOTE: This might take days. If you don't find the object in a short period of time, stop the exercise and come back to it the next day and try again. You may find the object immediately, a bit later, or not at all.

PART 2: TRUST

Lesson 11 – Trust yourself in challenge and fear

What does it mean to trust yourself in challenge and fear?

Sometimes a situation can look bleak, maybe even dire, and it seems that all help has disappeared. What do you do then?

A few years ago, I was traveling in Europe on a spiritual pilgrimage. I had intentionally left two weeks unplanned so that I could receive some spontaneous intuitive guidance about where to go. When my friend Lisa said, "You would love Malta," chills travelled down my arms, which is always a good sign for me.

But Malta? I had never thought of going there. When Lisa said Malta had many goddess temples and they were estimated to be over 10,000 years old, I started to get really excited. I bought my ticket that day.

When I told others on the tour about my choice of destination, they had a lot of opinions. "What are you going to Malta for?" someone asked. "Summer is the worst time of year to go." Someone else suggested that Scotland or Ireland might be better options, as the weather wouldn't be so hot. I started to doubt myself.

Why did I decide so quickly? Squirming in my seat on the tour bus, the image of the ticket in my purse flashed in my mind. *Maybe I could get a refund.*

In my meditation later that day, I imagined myself exchanging my ticket and going somewhere else. When I paid attention to how that felt, it was as if the inner workings of my chest had become disjointed. I knew this was telling me that exchanging my ticket was not the thing to do.

I decided to trust my initial inspiration and keep my ticket.

My trip to Malta turned out to be the most extraordinary part of my spiritual journey. I was very grateful that I had trusted myself.

Many years earlier, I did something I had felt called to do for several years: I started up my own business. I put together a simple plan, and it seemed achievable apart from the fact that I had very little money. As the weeks and months passed, I watched my bank account dwindle. I was desperate. How was I going to pay the bills?

Harassing thoughts began to plague me. *Maybe this isn't a good idea. You're not going to make it. You only did this so you could quit your job.*

I looked at my bank balance. *How am I going to pay the rent next month? How am I going to survive?*

Part of my inner dialogue tried to argue back. *But I am meant to do this.*

Really? You don't have anything to offer. Who do you think you are anyway?

I wanted to cry but no tears came. I closed my eyes, which were dry and sore from lack of sleep. I began to breathe deeply and slowly. My heartbeat slowed down as my body relaxed. Then I heard another voice inside me. It was gentle. *It's okay if you get a job to help you through this part. That doesn't mean failure.*

I opened my eyes. I had an idea. I could work on my business in the daytime, and in the evenings I could work in a restaurant. If my expenses were covered, I wouldn't be so anxious about selling my coaching and training services to corporate businesses.

Within two weeks, I had a job managing an Italian restaurant in the evenings. Within nine months, I had so much client work through my business that I had to quit my restaurant job.

That was over twenty years ago, and I haven't looked back since.

"Trusting yourself" is about listening to your own deep inner wisdom—which you can access through your intuition and meditation—rather than following your fears and judgements.

What might stop you from trusting yourself in challenge and fear?

When you don't slow down to breathe, you can't hear, feel or receive messages from your own deep wisdom.

When you feel, sense, see or hear the voice of your own deep wisdom and you let your conscious, fearful mind talk you out of following what you have heard, you can't benefit from your own inner guidance, which always knows what is in your best interest.

What are the benefits of trusting yourself in challenge and fear?

When I listen to and follow my own deep wisdom, I feel in the flow or in the zone even when I am in challenging situations. I feel more at peace inside.

I end up in the right place at the right time. No matter what is happening, things have a "rightness" to them—not from a moral or value-charged perspective, but from a "this is meant to happen" perspective.

Summary

- Trusting yourself means listening to and following your own deep inner wisdom, which you can access through your intuition and through meditation.

- When you slow down and breathe deeply into your belly, you can interrupt your fear and begin to access your inner wisdom.

- In moments of fear and challenge, it can take more effort to trust yourself, but doing so can lead you to a more fulfilling journey and outcome.

Exercise

This exercise guides you to pay attention to your inner feelings about a situation. The purpose of this is to practice slowing down and breathing, in order to access your inner wisdom.

STEPS

Step #1   Bring to mind a situation in your life that requires you to make a choice between two options.

Step #2   Take yourself somewhere where you can sit quietly for 15 minutes without interruption.

Step #3   Close your eyes and begin to breathe deeply and slowly into your belly. Do this for two minutes before moving on to step #4.

Step #4   Bring to mind the situation where you have a choice to make. Imagine yourself choosing one option. As you imagine this, observe the actions you are taking and notice how you feel inside while you take those actions.

Step #5   Then let go of those images. Take a few deep belly breaths without imagining anything. Do this for a few seconds.

Step #6   Bring to mind the situation where you have a choice to make. Imagine yourself choosing the other option. As you imagine this, observe the actions you are taking and notice how you feel inside while you take those actions.

Step #7   Then let go of those images. Take a few deep belly breaths without imagining anything. Do this for a few seconds.

Step #8   Write down your insights and notice what your inner wisdom is communicating about your options. Go ahead and make your choice or don't make your choice. The important part is at least you have more information from your own inner wisdom. You always have free will to make whatever choice you want.

PART 3: BE FREE

PART 3: BE FREE

Lesson 12 – Set yourself challenges to break through

What does it mean to set yourself challenges to break through?

You can set yourself challenges to overcome in many areas of life. Some examples are: physical challenges such as a health issue; personal challenges such as attending to an area of your life requiring attention but that you have avoided; and relationship challenges where you are disempowered.

This lesson is about setting yourself a challenge in an area of your life where you are disempowered and want to have a breakthrough.

I lived in New Zealand for many years, and during that time I travelled back to Canada every two years to visit with family. When I visited my mother, I always started off as a mature adult and slowly regressed into an annoyed, withholding, resentful teenager. By the time the visit came to an end, I inevitably felt ashamed of my behaviour.

A few years ago, I decided that I'd had enough of reverting back to old unhelpful habits each time I visited Mom, and I declared that I was going to have a breakthrough. I wanted to have a visit with my mom where I experienced love, connection and acceptance. That was my goal.

I also realised that if my goal was conditional upon my mom's behaviour changing, there would always be conflict between us, as I had learned from past experience that my efforts to change her never ended well.

I created a mantra for myself to help keep me on track. It went like this: "Mom doesn't have to do anything differently. I will keep my heart open and be in communication rather than get annoyed and go quiet." I knew this would be a challenge, but I was up for it.

During that visit, Mom and I decided to go shopping. "Is that all you're going to wear?" she asked.

Don't tell me what to wear! The thought was automatic as if I had not control. *Oh no. Here we go again!* I thought despairingly, noticing how quickly my old habit had been triggered.

I repeated my mantra to myself and took a slow, deep breath, bringing awareness into the centre of my chest. Instead of ignoring her and going quiet, I looked into her eyes and said, "What else do I need, Mom?"

"Well, with all that air-conditioning in the malls it's going to be cold. You might want to take a sweater."

"What a darn good idea," I said. And it was.

If I had continued to resist her, as I had done in the past, I would have ignored her comment, or been defensive. Then I'd feel guilty for being reactive. I would have been cold in the mall which would serve as a persistent reminder of how petty I had been—all the while pretending that everything was *fine*.

I breathed a deep sigh of relief. I'd had my first win.

Over the next few days, I had some losses but more wins. And as I continued to persevere, the wins began to win. I was breaking an old habit, and I was having a breakthrough.

When we set ourselves challenges to breakthrough it may be that numerous old habits stand in the way and the path might seem too daunting. Or maybe unhealed wounds reveal themselves that have previously held us back from dealing with this issue. A lot of fear and emotion can arise. Engaging a professional coach, counsellor or therapist for support through this healing process may be a wise choice.

What might stop you from setting challenges to break through?

The fulfilment of your goal will be inhibited if you require others to change their behaviour in any way.

Sometimes fear about how others will react causes us to hold back. If you get stuck in fear and don't take steps to become unstuck, it will stop you from breaking through old habits. Having fear is okay—we all do—but it doesn't have to stop you.

You won't break an old habit if you give up after your first failed attempt. In fact, giving up might itself be an old habit you want to break. If you feel like giving up, make perseverance part of your challenge.

When you break through an old habit, sometimes

it just goes away, but other times it keeps lurking. If you assume that having a breakthrough means you don't need to do any further work, you could be setting yourself up for a fall.

Breaking through a challenge is much easier if you have helpful support structures in place. Here are some possible sources of support: create a mantra for the challenge; tell someone you trust about your challenge and ask him or her to be a support person; write your challenge on your wall as an affirmation; or hire a professional coach to help you meet your goals with this.

What are the benefits of setting challenges to break through?

I feel empowered and positive, and my relationships change for the better.

I feel more authentic as I begin to have more honest conversations with others.

When I no longer have to cover up how I feel, I can be more present.

Summary

- "Setting yourself a challenge" means choosing an area in your life where you are not empowered, and challenging yourself to change an old habit in order to become more confident, enabled and strong in that area.

- You being empowered must not require anyone else to change.

- On the road to your breakthrough you will have some wins and some losses. Don't give up.

- Put in place a support structure to help you along your path of breaking through an old habit.

- If you get stuck in fear, or if the challenge you have set yourself involves confronting numerous old habits, it is wise to seek help from a professional.

- When you break old habits, you will feel more present, uplifted, strong inside and authentic.

Exercise

The intention of this exercise is to guide you to bring about empowering breakthroughs in your life.

NOTE: This exercise can be very confronting and takes a lot of courage. You might consider hiring a professional coach or therapist to support you as you take these steps.

STEPS

Step #1　Choose an area of your life where you want to be more empowered (in a particular circumstance or in your relationship with a specific person).

Step #2　Write down the behaviour and feelings *you* want to have in this situation without requiring anyone else around you to change. For example: *I want to feel connected and accepting with my mom.*

> **NOTE:** If I write down, *I want my mom to listen to me and be accepting of who I am*, it means that my mom has to change her behaviour. This won't work.

Step #3 Write down how you are going to be (your behaviours, your attitude, your response) in relation to that situation. For example: *I am going to keep my heart open and in communication instead of getting annoyed and going quiet.*

Step #4 Create a support structure that works for you. For example: create a mantra and say it often throughout the day, ask someone to be your support coach, or engage a professional coach.

Step #5 Keep a diary and make note of your observations and any changes in your thoughts, actions and words, no matter how small. This way you can track your progress.

Step #6 Give yourself positive feedback each time you make a step—even a tiny one—towards your goal.

NOTE: It's important to remember you may be breaking habits you have practiced for a long time. Making one small improvement is a feat. Giving yourself a lot of positive feedback will strengthen you during this process and help you to persist.

PART 3: BE FREE

Lesson 13 – Observe yourself and reflect deeply

What does it mean to observe yourself and reflect deeply?

First of all, it's important to note that observing yourself takes extensive effort. It is not an innate skill.

When you are "being" in the world, think about where your attention is. Your awareness is generally either focused on your own thoughts and feelings or on others and your interaction with them. Your consciousness is not usually directed toward observing yourself and the impact you are having on other people and your environment.

Actually, you can't observe yourself.

Imagine taking a video recording of yourself and then watching it. When you watch the recording, that's when you are able to self-observe. You see things you were not able to see at the time when the recording was taken. You might notice that your face makes expressions you didn't realise you made. Maybe the words you say in the recording don't come out the way you intended or the tone of your voice is different than you thought it was at the time.

In the moment of being, we are only conscious through our own eyes, from our own perspective.

"Observing yourself" means noticing how you occur to others, how your being and doing impacts the world around you. This requires deep inner reflection, and even then you can only imagine the impact you have.

I like to imagine that we are like waves in the ocean, each causing ripples and currents. It takes courage to be willing to see the impact of your waves.

Why is it important to do this? Observing yourself expands your capacity for compassion and for connection with others. It heals wounds and opens your consciousness.

Just the other day, I attended a workshop to make a medicine pouch—a small leather pouch that carries special herbs or other meaningful items such as crystals.

Everyone in the group was engrossed in hand sewing their pouches together. We were using glover needles, which have a triangular end with three sharp sides enabling the needle to pierce through leather. As I sewed, I began chatting with Jeanette, the indigenous woman who was facilitating the workshop. I shared with her that I had just moved back to Canada after 29 years and was learning a lot about indigenous culture, but that my learning curve had been steep.

I told her I recently met an indigenous elder who told me that the medicine drum represents the grandmother. I use a medicine drum in some of my workshops, and for the previous 12 months, which I'd spent on a road trip around the United States and Canada, I had left my drum in the cab of my truck when I wasn't using it. As a result, it slowly baked in the sun and wouldn't make sound anymore.

I told Jeanette that when I shared this with the elder, the elder looked at me with the same calm eyes she had held throughout our conversation and said, "Would you leave your grandmother in the car to overheat?"

It wasn't a question requiring an answer. It was intended to teach. The lesson was painful, as it opened my awareness to my lack of attention to caring for my hand-made drum.

I put down the piece of leather I was working on and looked at Jeanette, hoping that she would have a compassionate response to my story. She was unresponsive, but kept eye contact with me. I continued to share more, hoping to make some kind of connection with her.

I told her that a couple of weeks earlier I had been invited to attend a ceremonial sweat lodge. Having never been to a sweat lodge, I was very much looking forward to it. The morning of the ceremony, I awoke to a message on my cell phone from the organiser advising me that participants were required to abstain from alcohol for four days before attending a ceremony.

An email had been sent weeks earlier reminding participants of this, but I had missed it because I'd accepted the invitation only a few days before the event.

I'd had a glass of wine the evening before. I remembered picking up the glass to take a sip and something didn't feel right in my chest. I questioned whether I should have wine the day before a sweat lodge, but I didn't listen to my questioning. I told Jeanette about this experience as another example of a painful lesson I'd learned in my efforts to connect with indigenous culture.

When I'd finished telling her my story, I looked at her hoping for a response. Again she stayed silent, and there was nothing in her eyes letting me know that we had connected.

In a final attempt to create some kind of commonality between us I said, "My great grandmother is indigenous." This statement seemed to land between us, making the same kind of flat thud sound that my baked drum made.

She waited until I had nothing more to say and then politely moved on to speak with another participant. I had wanted to connect with her, but I felt as if I had achieved the opposite.

Baffled as to what happened in our interaction, I reflected on our conversation as I drove home that evening. I tried to put myself in her shoes, but how could I really? I hadn't experienced residential schools and the attempted destruction of my culture, but I did the best I could.

As I tried to imagine being her listening to a white settler talk about how hard it is to learn about another culture and hearing countless white settlers say they had some distant relative who was indigenous, the insights ripped open my heart.

Being in her shoes, I think I would feel indignant, invisible and have no desire to connect.

My hands moved further down the steering wheel. I wanted to crawl in a hole and pretend the conversation never happened. Then I spoke gently but firmly with myself. "Oh no you don't. You come back out and deal with this."

When I got home, I sat down at the computer. "Dear Jeanette," I wrote. "I want to apologise for some things I said today…" I shared with her my reflections and finished the letter with, "No reply is necessary, expected or hoped for." I realised that if she felt obliged to reply that would mean more emotional work for her to interact with me. I pressed the "send" button.

Her reply arrived in my inbox within an hour. She said that my letter had brought her to tears and that this was precisely the work for each of us to do: to reflect deeply on the impact of our words and our actions on each other.

Tears welled in my eyes as I read her reply. How beautiful to finally connect.

What might hinder you from observing yourself and reflecting deeply?

When you justify your actions by saying you didn't intend to have a negative impact, you deny the reality of how your actions have affected others and invalidate their feelings. You make it more difficult for your apology to be heard.

When we justify ourselves, we are usually looking to avoid being blamed. What we don't realise is that by justifying we bring blame into the conversation when there doesn't need to be any blame at all. When we can apologise without justifying, the blame often can disappear from both sides.

If you blame the other person for an uncomfortable interaction—for example, I could have decided that Jeanette was hard to connect with, shrugged it off and walked away—you have failed to acknowledge and learn from the impacts of your own behaviours and attitudes.

If you don't take the time to reflect on your own contributions to the challenges you face in relationships, you will feel less connected with others and with yourself.

If you notice these impacts but avoid taking responsibility—opting instead, for example, to be extra nice in an attempt to "make up" for what happened—this will lead to inauthentic communication, and you will miss out on opportunities to heal emotional wounds. This also contributes to the unease in relationship.

What are the benefits of observing yourself and reflecting deeply?

Even though you can never really know other people's circumstances or fully understand their life experiences, making the effort to imagine yourself in someone else's shoes opens your heart to compassion, which paves the road for more easeful and powerful communication.

When you deeply reflect on the possible impacts of your behaviour, you become more conscious of who you are in the world, and your ability to relate to others expands.

Summary

- Self-observation is not an innate skill. It takes concerted effort.

- Observing yourself means putting yourself in another person's shoes and deeply reflecting on the impact your behaviour might have had on them.

- It takes a lot of courage to observe yourself and deeply reflect.

- Ignoring an interaction that didn't feel right or minimising your awareness of your effect on others keeps you unconscious of your impact in the world.

- Being extra nice in an attempt to "make up" for your impact on others rather than directly addressing the impact leads to inauthentic communication.

- Observing yourself and deeply reflecting on and communicating your reflections to others creates greater awareness and connectedness with others and with yourself.

Exercise

The purpose of this exercise is to guide you through the steps of reflecting deeply and communicating with another about your reflections. To help you to focus on practicing the steps of this exercise, choose a circumstance with another person that is not a repetitive one or highly emotional.

NOTE: If in trying out these steps you uncover a lot of emotions, it may be helpful to engage the guidance of a trained professional.

STEPS

Step #1 Bring to mind a situation where an interaction with another person didn't feel right to you. Choose a situation that is not highly emotional or repetitive.

Step #2 Find a place where you can go for 30 minutes and not be disturbed. Think about the other person in the interaction, and bring to mind all of the things you know about that person's personal life history.

Step #3 Imagine yourself being that person and experiencing those things. Notice how it feels.

Step #4 Now bring to mind the interaction you had that didn't feel right. I imagine being the other person on the receiving end of your communication and your behaviour in that situation. Imagine this as best you can without judging or justifying your actions. Notice the thoughts and feelings you have being in the other person's shoes.

Step #5 Make note of your observations. Catch and interrupt self-judgments, as they are unhelpful.

Step #6 Communicate your insights to the other person. The door is now open for you to take action and communicate. This final step breaks the chains of old limiting habits that have caused pain and destruction in the world. These old limiting habits are based on the fear of being vulnerable with others and of how they might respond—a fear that has held humans back for generations and maintains dysfunction and sickness in our relationships.

NOTE: Find a way to communicate that does not put you in any danger. If it is truly unsafe to be with the other person, you might decide to write a letter and then burn it, allowing the communication to be heard by the universe.

You might also choose to work with a professional coach who has experience with these kinds of conversations.

Here is a simple format to follow for the communication:

1. If you are communicating in person, ask permission to have the conversation. For example, you might say, "I noticed a few things about myself in our interaction. Can I share them?"

2. "When I said / did……. I imagine you might have felt……"

3. "I am sorry."

Here are some guidelines to follow when having this conversation:

•   In this communication do not justify or explain

yourself at any point. If you do, the other person will mostly likely become defensive.

- Notice the words "I **imagine** you **might** have felt…" Using words that don't assume you know for sure allows room for the other person to feel however they feel, which might be close to what you said. The other person may or may not feel the need to say exactly what they felt, but most importantly it shows that you have made an effort to understand. Doing this opens the door to healing.

- It might happen that the other person responds in a way that indicates the situation wasn't important to them and that it didn't matter. Don't take this personally. People aren't always willing to say how they feel. If they respond like this, simply shrug and say something like, "Well, I'm sorry" and say nothing more. Trust that your words have made a difference. You might notice the person being more open towards you.

PART 3: BE FREE

Lesson 14 – Hold the vision and let go of the plan

What does hold the vision and let go of the plan mean?

This lesson first came to me in a meditation. I had been on a spiritual pilgrimage, and through various meditations I kept getting the message that it was *time for me to fly*. I wondered what this actually meant, and I decided to ask a master: the eagle.

Sitting on the ledge of a big rock in Sedona with my eyes closed, I relaxed into a meditative state. I telepathically put out a call for Eagle, and in my mind I saw a very large eagle land on the ledge just above me. The vision in my mind rolled out like a dream:

> *"Eagle, will you teach me how to fly?"*
>
> *Eagle glanced at me and nodded. Then it looked straight ahead for a moment, as if contemplating where to start. It communicated with me telepathically in thought forms.*
>
> *"First, never take off unless you know where you are going."* What a good point, I thought.

"Once you are in the air, stay alert as you look for opportunities, and be flexible enough to change course if an opportunity arises."

Another vision appeared before me of a bird flying towards a branch. It spotted an insect and immediately darted towards the insect, then flew on, landing on a different branch than the one it had originally aimed for.

I imagined how ridiculous it would be if birds always had to end up at the destinations they aimed for. I envisaged them bumping into each other, unable to alter their course, making redundant flights with the sole purpose of landing on their original targets.

I was stunned by the simplicity and depth of this lesson. And I was challenged by how to interpret it, because my human logic told me that it was fickle to change my course every time a better opportunity arose.

Spreading its wings, Eagle lifted up to fly, leaving me with one last message.

"Hold the vision. Let go of the plan."

Then it flew off.

As humans, we create plans to accomplish things, and having plans means having expectations about *how* we will get to the outcomes we desire. This makes logical sense, but when we expand our consciousness and work more with our intuition, we are dealing with a different kind of wisdom.

This lesson is about letting go of your plans. I'm not suggesting that you shouldn't make plans or that that you should aimlessly wander about hoping things will happen. It's about being willing to let go of the plans you have made in order to open yourself to the possibilities and opportunities that show themselves along your path.

"Hold the vision" of where you are going, but let go of the plan.

The word "vision" here doesn't have to mean a big vision for your life, your business or the world—and yet it might. The word "vision" in this lesson means a visual image of the outcome you want, big or small. As you hold this in your mind, pay attention to the steps that appear before you and take them. Often these steps are ones you could not have planned for or anticipated in the beginning.

As I began my twelve-month road trip across North America I also started writing my second book (this one you are reading now). My vision was to tour with both books the following year. I was excited as the scope of the book took shape.

I was usually travelling for one to three days and then I would stay somewhere for a few days before moving on again. My days were a mixture of driving all day, finding a place to sleep the night, setting up camp, preparing meals, exploring, meeting and visiting with new people, planning my travels and sleeping.

I had less and less time to write.

I tried to fit the writing in every spare moment I had, but those moments were also needed to do laundry or maintenance work on the camper. Eventually I put the writing aside feeling disappointed, not knowing how I was going to finish it.

But I still kept a clear vision in my mind of touring the next year.

Then something strange started to happen. Mostly I had been sleeping well, but I began waking up at 4:30 every morning with no alarm. The first time it happened on my travels, I opened my eyes and turning over to look at the time on my cell phone I wondered why I felt so awake. Then I heard a whisper in my mind, "Write." I smiled. This was how I had written my first book—in the early hours of the morning. I reached for my computer.

The first draft of my second book was finished in two months.

After 12-months of travel, I still felt drawn to stay on tour, but I needed a different vehicle. My ¾ ton pick-up truck with a truck camper attached was 24 feet long and just over 12 feet high—far too cumbersome to manoeuvre in cities. Finding parking and places to stay the night was sometimes impossible so I tended to avoid the metropolitan areas.

But the next part of my tour was taking me into the cities to attend networking meetings and other speaking engagements. I needed to sell the truck and the camper.

I started to feel some anxiety. Summer had already arrived and many people who wanted this kind of vehicle would have already bought one. Once fall arrives in Canada, people put their campers in storage. If my camper didn't sell this summer it would have to wait for next summer. I needed it to sell to have money to purchase my next vehicle. I didn't have the time to wait for next summer.

Along the roadsides over the past couple of months, I had driven by countless truck campers and caravans displaying "for sale" signs. Some looked new, others looked used, while several more were plain run down. I wondered how long they'd been sitting there, "for sale". Would mine be one of them?

I shook my head as if to shake out the images of memories flashing before me and I created in my mind the vision of my truck and camper being sold easily. I even started saying, "I'll sell them by the end of the month."

I had options for selling them. I could sell the truck and camper together or separately, listing them on the online auction in Ontario. Or I could take the camper back to the RV retailer where I first purchased it and use the truck as a trade-in for my next vehicle.

Several friends were encouraging me to sell them on my own. I would make more money and it was *easy* they said. Selling the camper on my own posed the problem of where to stand it so that people could view it. I couldn't leave it on the street and I didn't have a driveway for it.

I sat down to meditate on each of the options. When I imagined myself taking the camper back to the RV retailer, I felt calmer inside my chest compared with the other options.

The RV retailer agreed to take the camper back on consignment, meaning that I would get paid when someone purchased it and he would take a percentage. "We'll call you as soon as anyone is interested." As I walked away from the dealership I noticed they had a lot of caravans and campers—more than they had the previous year. I started to doubt my choice.

> *What if it doesn't se...?*
>
> *Nope!*
>
> *But what if...?*
>
> *Nope!*

I was not going to let myself even think about any other outcome. *The camper and the truck are going to sell easily by the end of the month.* That was 3 weeks away. I held the vision.

One week went by. No phone call. Twelve days passed. Not a word.

I was feeling uneasy. Taking a moment to meditate on it, an idea came to me to check out where they had my camper advertised. As I searched the inventory on their website I saw the simple advertisement for my camper. Right above my listing was a bigger, bolder advertisement including a video tour for a brand new truck camper that looked a lot like mine. It was selling for only one thousand dollars more than my second hand one. *They are out to sell that camper. Not mine.*

Then I thought to check if they had advertised my camper on the large, public online auction site. They hadn't. I suspected the majority of customers would search the online auction first. Without any time to spare I posted an advertisement for my camper.

The next day I got a phone call about the camper. Within 48 hours I had sold the camper. The RV dealer waived their commission and I had more money in my hand than I would have had I sold through the dealer.

By the end of the month I had found my next vehicle and had negotiated a lucrative trade-in price for my pick-up truck facilitated by the car salesperson wanting to meet end-of-month sales targets.

What might stop you from holding the vision and letting go of the plan?

If you don't have a vision of where you are going or what you want to create, life can feel purposeless.

If you create a detailed plan and force yourself to stick to it, you might miss out on the universe contributing to the fulfilment of your vision.

If you get stuck in limiting thoughts and doubt that your vision can be realised, you send mixed messages to the universe and interrupt the flow of fulfilling your desires.

What are the benefits of holding the vision and letting go of the plan?

When I hold my vision, let go of my plan and take the steps that appear before me, things happen more easily. Miracles occur.

When I am not spending energy trying to make what happens fit with the details of my plan, I feel less stress.

As I hold the vision and allow unexpected happenings to occur, welcoming them as part of the path, an outcome that is even better than what I originally imagined can manifest.

Summary

- Don't act until you know where you are going.

- Hold in your mind a visual image of the outcome you want.

- Stay alert to opportunities along the way and take them even if it alters the course you planned.

- Letting go of the plan doesn't mean you wander aimlessly hoping things will happen.

- Forcing yourself to stick to your plan can prevent you from being open to opportunities presented by the universe that can contribute to the fulfilment of your vision.

- When you hold the vision and let go of the plan, miracles can happen.

Exercise

Sometimes having a physical representation of your vision can help you to "hold the vision." For example, when I was writing my book, I mocked up the cover page of the book and posted it on my wall. If your vision is the outcome of a multi-faceted project, you might want to create a vision board. A vision board consists of a large piece of paper with various images from magazines and maybe drawn images that together represent the various aspects of your vision.

Other examples of physical visual representations could be: a piece of art, a painting, a toy or written words. Whatever you choose, it should remind you of the outcome you want, which will remind you to keep holding the vision.

The purpose of this exercise is to create your own visual representation of your vision.

STEPS

Step #1   Write down on paper all the aspects of a vision you have.

Step #2   Choose the physical representation you want to use: vision board, physical object, graphic image, piece of art, etc.

Step #3   Gather the materials you need.

Step #4   Make the physical visual representation.

Step #5   Put the representation in a place where you will easily notice it every day.

Step #6   As you "hold the vision," pay attention to the ideas that come to your mind, be open to the opportunities that arise and choose whether or not to take them.

PART 3: BE FREE

Lesson 15 – Release all hopes, desires, dreams and expectations

What does release all hopes, desires, dreams and expectations mean?

These words have been used in various ways in different personal development practices and by different individuals. My suggestion for this lesson is that you put aside your current understanding of these words and allow yourself to open to the ways they are being used here—like trying on a new jacket and noticing how and where it fits.

Let's explore the meanings of these words for this lesson.

"I hope things work out." "I hope things get better." "I hope they like me." "I hope that doesn't happen." Life is full of hopes—wanting things to go a particular way.

Inherent in the experience of hope is the desire for something to be *better* than what it is. This makes it challenging to be with circumstances in whatever form they arise whether better, worse, unexpected or indifferent and can lead to suffering.

Having desires and dreams is similar to having hope.

Although having them isn't bad, in fact, our desires

and dreams often guide us to create wonderful things, but when we cling to them, when we compare what is with what we think *should* be, when we *expect* particular outcomes and base our satisfaction on the fulfilment of our desires and dreams, this also leads to suffering. Having expectations can be particularly dissatisfying. An expectation comes with a benchmark that must be reached in order for satisfaction to be fulfilled.

Hopes, desires, dreams and expectations all involve wanting something that doesn't exist in the present moment, which can lead to feelings of dissatisfaction with the now. To release hopes, desires, dreams and expectations is to let go of the internal state of wanting.

This might seem to contradict Lesson 14—Hold the vision and let go of the plan—as Lesson 14 is about *holding on* and this lesson is about *releasing,* but they actually can work together.

Let's say you want to find a life partner. That is a *vision* you hold. And you have a checklist of all the qualities you want that person to have. These are *hopes, desires, dreams and expectations*. Go ahead and put together the checklist if that is what you want to do, but then release it. Holding on to it comparing every potential candidate you meet with each point on your list creates a more critical approach, one that might not be pleasant for either of you.

You could also end up missing out on meeting someone with whom you are well matched because they don't look like you expected, don't have all the qualities you were hoping for, but they have other characteristics you hadn't thought of.

Holding on to your hopes, desires, dreams and expectations can create internal stress as you attempt to make the external environment fit what you want.

Releasing hopes, desires, dreams and expectations is a technique that can be used moment by moment.

Several years ago, I planned to move back to Canada from New Zealand. I had sold everything, and my bags were packed. Then I met a man and fell in love. But there was a problem. He lived in New Zealand, and I was moving. The more time we spent together, the more I wanted to be with him.

Richard and I were in his back yard sitting by the fire pit. I watched as he mindfully broke branches and placed pieces of wood skilfully in a mound. He was creating a fire—for us. I could feel my chest exploding with love for him.

My thoughts shifted to my impending move, and suddenly my heart was aching. Tears filled my eyes. How could I walk away from this? This was the relationship I had been dreaming of for such a long time.

My fingers gripped the rock I was sitting on. Feelings of dread filled my chest. My forehead tightened with worry. Not a good start to what was supposed to be a romantic and enjoyable evening.

Then I remembered my new mantra. I closed my eyes and whispered, "I release all hopes, desires, dreams and expectations." My body relaxed immediately. I stopped agonising inside and let go of pushing away and clutching at potential futures. All the tension and worry disappeared—like magic. I could breathe more easily.

I was present again.

I opened my eyes. Richard was looking at me. I smiled and felt the warm flow in my heart again. In that moment, I was in love, and I was going to have a beautiful evening.

What might stop you from releasing all hopes, desires, dreams and expectations?

Fear of not getting what you want, or fear of losing what you already have can keep you holding on. Fear can stop you but it doesn't have to.

What are the benefits of releasing all hopes, desires, dreams and expectations?

When I release all hopes, desires, dreams and expectations, my inner state changes. I free myself from rejecting what is and grasping after what is not. I am present in this moment. When I am present, I have access to a more resourceful, conscious state where I can make wiser, more empowered choices. My mind is more creative, I feel more joy, and options for action are more easily available.

Summary

- To hope, desire, dream or expect means to want something to turn out a particular way, which can lead to suffering.

- Projecting fear onto a potential future situation

keeps you in a state of worry where you are unable to enjoy the moment or access resourceful thinking.

- Releasing hopes, desires, dreams and expectations means letting go of the internal state of wanting.

- When you release all hopes, desires, dreams and expectations, you relax and stop resisting what is or longing for what is not.

- This helps you to live in the present moment with more peace, make wiser choices, and cultivate the inner resources to be more resilient.

Exercise

The purpose of this exercise is to guide you through the simple steps of practicing this technique in areas of your life that cause you suffering.

STEPS

Step #1   Identify a situation in your life that you are not happy with.

Step #2   Bring that situation to mind and notice how you feel inside.

Step #3   Close your eyes. Focus on that situation and say the mantra out loud, "I release all hopes, desires, dreams and expectations." Say this a few times slowly so that you can feel each word as you say it.

Step #4   Keep your eyes closed and notice how you feel inside. Breathe slowly and deeply as you let the feelings come and sit with them for a few moments.

Step #5   Notice if it feels easier to release one aspect as compared with another. For example, maybe you feel resistance inside when you say the words: *I release all hopes,* and when you say the word: *expectations,* it feels easier and you relax. Write down your observations and insights.

Step #6   Open your eyes. If it feels right, take action to step into the experience of having let go and being more present. This action might be to simply enjoy the moment you are in, or it might be to complete a specific task.

Step #7   Repeat these steps as often as you like.

PART 3: BE FREE

Lesson 16 – Heal self-compromise and reclaim your power

What does heal self-compromise and reclaim your power mean?

The word *compromise* has two distinct meanings, although we often collapse them together. One meaning of compromise is 'to leave something open to danger and make vulnerable.' For example: *The poor structural design compromised the apartment building, which now suffers from internal leaking.*

The other meaning of *compromise* is 'to settle differences by mutual consent and to let go of opposing desires.' For example: *My husband and I were disagreeing on our house redecorating until we finally compromised. He agreed to the green colour I wanted to paint the living room and I agreed to the piece of artwork he wanted to put in the hallway. A work example could be: My manager asked me to work some extra hours on a project which I didn't want to do. But I said I would do the work if she gave me an extra week holiday time. She agreed. We both compromised and I was satisfied with that.*

In everyday language, it isn't always clear which of these two meanings is intended, and often the word is used with both meanings at once: an agreement between parties and feeling at risk or vulnerable about that agreement, and therefore unsatisfied with it.

When we make an agreement with someone that involves letting go of something we wanted, sometimes we feel at peace about it, like in the above examples. For the purposes of this lesson, I will call this *negotiation and agreement*.

However when we let go of something we wanted in order to make an agreement and we feel dissatisfied or uncomfortable in some way, for the purposes of this lesson I will call this *self-compromise*.

The feeling of dissatisfaction usually manifests because we have given up something of high importance or value to us. Often this value is something that supports us personally: mentally, emotionally, physically or spiritually. I refer to this as a *personal value*. When we give up a personal value, it is often driven by fear—usually fear of losing something else that we value.

Many people believe that they have to compromise themselves in relationships, but this is not true. *Negotiation and agreement* are necessary, but the moment you compromise yourself, problems will follow.

When I was working on the first draft of my first book, I created a morning routine that usually involved waking up at 4:30 a.m., meditating, writing, saying prayers and going for a walk. This had become my ritual for greeting the day. Doing this routine is one of my personal values. It helps me to feel grounded and clear inside.

Several months after creating this supportive

daily routine, I was in a new relationship. While the relationship was exciting and enriching in many ways, I realised that I hadn't been doing my morning ritual with any regularity for weeks. My attention had turned to attending to Richard's needs. My book wasn't getting written and I didn't feel happy with myself.

I'd been in this situation before in other relationships and it didn't feel very good. Something was at the source of my self-compromise and I couldn't see it yet.

One morning as Richard and I lay in bed, the song of chirping birds called me, and I opened my eyes. I glanced over at Richard's face. His eyes were still closed. I felt the desire to get up and do my morning ritual, but I didn't move. I told myself that if I got out of bed early he would feel neglected and would eventually not want to be in a relationship with me.

A niggle of resentment stirred inside me, and the chatter in my head started up: *It's much easier not being in a relationship. I can do what I want and not worry if I am pleasing someone else.*

As I looked over at him sleeping next to me, an insight began to unravel. I hadn't checked in with him if he expected me to stay in bed with him all morning. He had no idea what was going on in my head, and I was busy making assumptions about what was going on in his.

Then the crack of insight got bigger. *This is how I do it! This is how I compromise myself.* I didn't even need him to be involved. I did all the self-compromising on my own while assuming what he was thinking.

It wasn't until I reflected on what was underneath the surface of the self-compromise that I saw how I had repeated this pattern in failed relationship after failed relationship. Over time, I became more and more resentful about the ways in which I was compromising myself, but I didn't say anything until the bitterness had closed my heart. When I finally ended those relationships, relieved that I no longer had to live with so much self-compromise, it never occurred to me that the cause was my own assumptions—based on an old fear of being abandoned.

Pondering this deep revelation, I felt something release inside. Then I did some healing work with this old fear. As I brought to mind the fear, I saw a four-year-old child—my inner, wounded child who felt abandoned. That part of me would do anything to not be abandoned again, such as compromise something that was important.

I imagined myself holding her and reassuringly telling her, *It's going to be okay. I've got you now. I won't leave you, ever.* This was what I had wanted Richard to tell me, but really it was me who needed to hear it from me! Warmth spread through my whole chest. I felt alive and excited. I could hardly wait to share my insights with Richard.

Richard opened his eyes and smiled at me lovingly. My heart flipped, and in the next second I gasped with fear. I was afraid of losing him. *Don't say anything,* whispered the four-year-old.

I visualised the wise woman in my heart holding the hand of the four-year-old, and in my mind said to her,

I have to.

I looked at Richard and clenched my palms. The fear shook my voice but I didn't let it stop me. "I want to tell you about an insight I just had." My heart pounded and tears filled my eyes but I kept going. I told him everything: my thoughts, my fears and my realisations. As I continued to speak, the fear shifted to relief and then to a sense of deep inner strength, and in that strength I no longer feared how he would respond.

I reclaimed my power.

I did this by contemplating deeply on questions such as: Why am I making it his fault that I'm not doing what's important to me? Where else have I done this? What am I really afraid of? And then I shared my insights. The door was now open for me to re-establish my morning ritual, and with it the value I place on taking care of myself.

When I finished speaking, Richard pulled back the bed covers. "Go do your routine," he said. "The more you do what you want, the more you are going to love me."

What might stop you from healing self-compromise and reclaiming your power?

When you blame others for your inability to be yourself, you are setting yourself up to live with unhappiness in your relationships and in your heart.

Doing the work to heal the fear inside is part of reclaiming your power. When you take the time to find the wounded child inside of you, healing can be as simple as it was in my story: imagine yourself holding that child and saying what he or she is longing to hear. Not doing this healing work can lead you to repeat the same pattern again and again.

It takes courage to speak out for what is really important to you in the face of fear. And when you hold back and don't speak out, you can keep yourself caught in the trap of self-compromise, which always feels dissatisfying.

In order to justify not speaking out, sometimes we tell ourselves that what we want isn't really important, but over time resentment grows. Emotional pressure can build inside leading to possible explosive or inappropriate responses, often blaming the other person.

What are the benefits of healing self-compromise and reclaiming your power?

When I do the work to find and heal the wounded child inside, I set myself free from old habits and chains of the past.

I create the possibility of more fulfilling relationships.

I build my confidence and experience more self-love.

When I share my feelings and insights with others, it can open up empowering conversations which can lead to stronger, healthier relationships.

NOTE: If you choose to have these conversations, depending on the circumstances, it can be wise to work with a professional coach to help prepare you.

Summary

- Negotiation and agreement is different from compromising yourself. It is often necessary to let go of things that we want, but whether this amounts to negotiation or self-compromise depends on what we are letting go of and how we feel about it.

- Sometimes you let go of something highly important to you that supports you in some way: mentally, emotionally, physically or spiritually. When you do this, it is usually driven by fear.

- Reflecting on your patterns of self-compromise rather than continuing to blame others can open the door to insight.

- Finding the fear inside and doing the work to heal the fear, is the first step to setting yourself free and reclaiming your power.

- Communicating insights about how you have compromised yourself can be part of interrupting old habits of holding back, and this can also be a powerful step to reclaiming your inner power.

- It can be wise to work with a professional coach to help prepare you for these conversations if you choose to have them.

Exercise

It can take courage to admit that you feel resentment. The intention of this exercise is to explore the self-compromise hidden underneath feelings of resentment and to open the door to reclaiming your inner power in that area.

For example, let's say you are at work and it's lunch time. You have a pre-arranged lunch meeting with a friend. Half an hour before you leave to meet your friend, your manager asks you to do a favour for her. It needs to be done right away. She says it will only take one hour, although you know it will take two hours. You didn't mind the first time she asked you for something like this—just before lunch—because you like to be helpful. You didn't mind the second time, either. But now you feel a little bit annoyed (hint: resentment). You take a deep breath and say, "Sure." You cancel your lunch date and get to work.

There are many reasons why you may experience resentment. Justifying it, pretending you don't feel it or ignoring it, doesn't make it go away. The resentment is still there. You just might not feel it as much. Then the next time something happens when you compromise yourself once more, the feeling of resentment will arise again, often a little stronger than the time before.

The resentment is the tip of the iceberg, and it is worth exploring what's underneath. It takes courage to look there, but when you do, there is an opportunity for you to take responsibility, reclaim your inner power and dissolve your resentment.

Delving underneath your resentment can be a deep diving journey, one you might wisely choose to do with a trained professional. The steps in this exercise are **not** designed for deep exploration; rather, they are meant to inspire reflection about how you came to compromise yourself and how you might begin to take your inner power back.

Completing Step #1 might take a day or two of paying attention as you go through your day to identify a feeling of resentment.

STEPS

Step #1   Identify an area in your life where you feel resentful (for example, when you agree to do something that you don't want to do, like in the example above). At first, it might be not be easy to identify feelings of resentment. It doesn't have to be something big. It might be a situation that is very small, or *seems* very small.

Step #2   Take an hour and find a place where you can sit quietly without being disturbed. Make sure you have a pen and paper with you.

Step #3   Close your eyes. Breathe deeply into your belly for one minute.

Step #4   Bring to mind the situation where you have feelings of resentment. Ask yourself these questions and write down the answers:

- What am I feeling resentful about?

- What am I not doing that I want to do (or doing that I don't want to do)?

- Who am I blaming, and what am I blaming them for?

- What am I afraid will happen?

- What does the other person not know about my situation and about what's important to me?

Step #5   What are your observations about your answers? Write down your insights.

Step #6   Reflect on what it is you are not doing that you want to do or what you are doing that you don't want to do. This is probably connected to a personal value that you are compromising (mine was a morning routine that supported me to feel grounded, clear and healthy). Put words to what is important to you and write it down.

Step #7   Explore and write down your answers to these questions:

- Why is this personal value important to you?

- How does this personal value support you?

Step #8   Reflect on things you could do or say to take steps towards fulfilling this personal value and no longer compromising yourself. (For example, I chose to share my insights with Richard knowing this would create opportunity to re-establish my morning routine.)

Step #9   There are many actions you *could* take. Choose the actions you *will* take to reclaim your power in this area.

NOTE: Working with a professional coach to assist you taking action with this exercise can be very helpful.

PART 3: BE FREE

Lesson 17 – Dare to love yourself

What does it mean to dare to love yourself?

For many people, this is the most challenging lesson by far.

When I was four years old, I used to spend a lot of time outside in our backyard talking with my closest friends—the trees and the rocks. I remember having meaningful conversations about life, not that I can recall any of the content now, but the feeling of love and acceptance in those conversations has remained with me. I still talk with trees and rocks.

My dad used to call me "Doddling Daughter," meaning that I was slow. I would often become so engrossed with whatever I was doing in the moment—talking with an insect, for example—that I would forget about the time. The nickname might sound endearing, but often it came with punishment. As I write this, a memory flashes before me of my little fingers being slammed in the car door because I wasn't quick enough to get into the car. Dad, in his haste and blinded by his anger that we were leaving late, had shut the door without looking.

Dad had high standards—his own harsh self-criticisms projected onto others—and I never met them.

I wasn't quick enough, smart enough, talented enough, confident enough. I wasn't anything enough.

At twelve, I had a growth spurt. I was leggy and not very coordinated. "Why aren't you like the other girls who are more active and get involved in sports?" my dad asked. As usual, I wanted to please him, but I couldn't. I wasn't quick on my feet. I wasn't good with a ball. I preferred being alone in my bedroom reading spiritual and science fiction books.

Maybe dad's right, I thought. *Maybe I should try gymnastics.* I had little confidence in my body and couldn't imagine hurling it sideways to do a cartwheel, but I took a deep breath and went to one of the classes. As I sat on the bench and watched what the other girls were doing, the excitement built in my belly, and I decided that next time I would participate.

I could hardly wait to get home to tell dad. "You watched?" he said. "Is that all? You didn't *do* anything!" My smile disappeared, and I bit my lip to hold back the stinging tears.

As I grew up, I began taking on my father's criticisms, showing myself no compassion and little patience.

When I was in my late teens, I suffered from a version of anorexia. I scowled as I looked at my body in the mirror. I pinched my thighs. *You're ugly. Look how big your thighs are.* In fact I was very slim and always had been, but I couldn't see it. I had this image in my mind of the perfect body I was supposed to possess. I believed that if I had a perfect body, I would be enough. I would be loved and accepted. But until I had achieved perfection,

I was unworthy.

I stopped eating for days at a time. I was on a mission to be perfect. But it was like holding my breath—I could only do it for so long, and then I gasped for air. After a few days, the hunger gnawed at me, and I could no longer resist. I sat down to a block of cheese, a loaf of bread and some lettuce—a token vegetable—and ate it all in one sitting. There was something satisfying about eating it all in the moment fulfilling my fantasies but then that feeling of disgust in myself always followed.

I had become my own tormentor, constantly reminding myself of my lack of worth, criticising every mistake I made. The thought of taking care of myself and putting myself first almost seemed dangerous! Not only was I not worth putting first but it threatened my goal of becoming perfect in order to please my dad and earn his love and acceptance.

I know that mine is a common story. So many of us suffer from a lack of self-worth. All around me I notice the symptoms, which swing like a pendulum, from a lack of self-care to an over-obsession of self-care—two sides of the same coin. Some of these symptoms include: self-criticism, over-achieving, under-achieving, self-harm, abusive relationships, harmful eating habits, overworking, putting others first and paying little attention to our own needs or obsessively attending only to our own needs—often being unaware of others.

My erratic eating habits carried on until my 30s. Numerous times I got myself motivated and tried to eat better and do some exercise but each time I gave up. After the initial energy burst, my interest waned and the effort seemed too much.

Then when I started my business coaching other people to live empowering lives, I had to deal with what wasn't working in my own. If I didn't, then I couldn't help others deal with their challenges. I couldn't help others unless I helped myself.

I began doing emotional healing work with the wounded parts inside of me: the three year old and the twelve year old. (I cover more extensively about healing old emotional wounds in Lesson 6 – Do the work: take responsibility and heal emotional wounds.) And I decided to deal with the ongoing issues of eating poorly and not exercising.

My new routine went like this: I scheduled in my diary when to eat to make sure I had three good meals a day. I created a morning self-care routine consisting of a hot lemon drink, meditation and exercise. In order to get everything done before work, I set my alarm for 5:30 a.m.

Sticking to my new routine wasn't easy. Some days were harder than others.

The loud buzzing of my alarm startled me. With an automatic arm movement, I reached over and turned it off. Leaning back, I closed my eyes again in the dark, peace and quiet. My body felt heavy and tired. It didn't want to go to the gym. I wanted to sleep more. *What's the point? I never keep a routine anyway. What's the use of starting something I'm only going to give up? Why not give up now?* My thoughts were seductively luring me back into slumber. I knew if I lay there long enough, it would soon be too late to do my routine. Then I wouldn't have to be responsible for taking care of myself.

But that morning, a force within me stirred and I sat bolt upright. I had been here before and this time I was not going to give up on myself. "Get up! Get up!" I shouted, commanding my body and throwing back the bedcovers.

After the first week of keeping my routine, I started to feel good. Several weeks on, I was feeling really good. Months later, I felt strong in my body and more confident in myself. Years on, I can't imagine living any other way.

But this road was not a straight one. Some days were still challenging. As I continued with my self-care routine, I discovered more layers of self-abuse and learned more ways to love myself. I began to listen to guided meditations on self-love, say loving affirmations to myself first thing in the morning and before going to bed, and kept a daily gratitude journal of things I was grateful to myself for.

On my third day practicing gratitude writing, I sat up in bed, my fingers poised above my diary. I looked at the clock. 11:00 p.m. I had been sitting there for half an hour, and I still hadn't written anything. I sighed. *Come on.* I whined at myself. *There must be something. I'm tired.* I hadn't done anything I was proud of that day. I hadn't called the client I'd meant to call. I still hadn't finished the proposal another client was waiting for. I hadn't booked a venue for the next round of lunch-hour presentations. The unruly pile of receipts was still waiting in my drawer for me to sort through. I'd forgotten to show up for my massage appointment, which I would probably have to pay for. The bag of shoes destined for the shoe repair was still sitting by the front door. I'd spent all day working on my presenter notes for a one-hour talk. Overall, not very satisfying.

One of the signs of being caught in self-criticism is when you notice all the things you haven't done and the mistakes you have made rather than paying attention to what you have accomplished.

I contemplated closing the diary and calling it a day. *Just this once. I'll write in it tomorrow.* But I wouldn't let myself. I was very familiar with the conversation I was having in my head. This was how I slowly gave up on things, and I wasn't going to do that. I needed to look deeper and listen.

I put aside my impatient thoughts and began breathing deeply and slowly in my heart, putting myself in a relaxed, meditative state. I then asked, *What am I grateful to myself for today?*

At first there was silence. Then as I listened patiently, I heard a quiet voice in my heart say, *You finished the notes for your talk. That's going to be a good talk.*

That's right. And it is going to be a really good presentation. I felt good about the work I had done. I wrote that down and closed my eyes again. Breathing deeply, I asked my heart once more, *What else am I grateful to myself for today?*

You took breaks in the day and ate your lunch. You took care of yourself.

I did. Tears flowed to my eyes.

You rescheduled the meeting with the accountant a week in advance rather than leaving it to the last minute.

When your massage therapist called to let you know you missed your appointment, you didn't justify yourself with some long explanation that isn't helpful to anyone. You simply apologised from your whole heart and booked another appointment.

You drank your two litres of water today, which is a real accomplishment.

I was on a roll.

And you didn't stay stuck in this exercise and close the diary. You meditated and took yourself further.

Loving yourself is a daring act. It requires great courage to go beyond the battlefield of the knives of criticism. It requires a warrior-for-love's determination to break the spell of lethargic resignation from years of practiced unworthiness.

What might hinder you from daring to love yourself?

Listening to and being guided by your own self-sabotaging thoughts, rather than accessing your inner wisdom, will get in the way of loving yourself.

Staying stuck in self-criticism and focusing your attention on what you didn't do and the mistakes you made keeps you in a cycle of self-abuse. But we can heal our self-criticising thoughts and let go of them completely.

What are the benefits of daring to love yourself?

When I break through old patterns and love myself, I feel fantastic and worthy.

Interrupting self-criticism and shifting to a positive perspective of myself makes me feel empowered and respected.

Finding the courage to interrupt self-sabotaging thoughts and taking actions of self-love makes me feel loved and nurtured.

Summary

- To avoid judgement and punishment, we learn to please others.

- Many of us grow up being criticised and learn to criticise ourselves.

- It requires great courage and determination to break habits of criticism and fear.

- Interrupting self-sabotaging thoughts and instead taking actions to care for yourself can feel loving and nurturing.

Exercise

There are many exercises you can use to develop self-love. Meditation is first on my list, as it helps to open your heart. If you haven't already, I suggest putting in place a daily meditation practice, no matter how brief. (See the NOTE below for some meditation guidelines.)

The intention of the exercise in this lesson is to help shift the attention of the mind away from self-criticism and towards a healthier, caring and loving perspective of yourself. It involves keeping a self-gratitude journal.

STEPS

Step #1   Find a dedicated journal to use for this purpose.

Step #2   Set aside about 30 minutes each day to write in your journal. Choose a time in the day that works for you. Maybe last thing before bed, or at lunch time, or at the end of the work day.

Step #3   Write down five things you are grateful to yourself for that day. If you find yourself stuck, interrupt all self-critical thoughts and take a few minutes to meditate. Then breathe into the centre of your chest and ask yourself: *What's one thing I did today that I am grateful for?* (Reread the last story in this chapter to inspire you if you need help.)

Step #4   When you have written down five things, close your journal, put it to your heart and say, "Thank you," to yourself.

NOTE: If you find it difficult to bring compassion to yourself, pretend you are speaking lovingly to a close friend or to a child as you do this exercise.

NOTE: Here are some guidelines for meditating.

You don't need any special techniques to meditate. Simply find a space to sit quietly and undisturbed for the length of time you set—perhaps five or ten minutes. Close your eyes and begin breathing deeply and slowly in your belly. Choose something to put your attention on, such as, your breath going in and out of your nose.

It doesn't mean that your attention will automatically stay there. The mind wanders. This is the whole practice of meditation. Instead of interacting with your thoughts, let them be there and, simply move your attention back to your breath. You may need to do this many times during your meditation.

Epilogue

I completed this book mostly in the early mornings during a period in my life when it seemed there wasn't enough time to write another book. But—thanks to some of the lessons in this self-coaching guide—time was not an issue.

I loved writing this book. May you find value for yourself and your life on these pages as I have.

If you are interested in exploring further work with me, go to my website to find out about the courses, retreats and coaching I offer: www.leannebabcock.ca.

Acknowledgements

Firstly, I thank you, the reader, the brave warrior of your heart, for daring to face your inner dragons and open yourself to the truly wild and extraordinary being you are. My heart expands beyond all borders with gratitude to you for doing your own personal development work to heal your wounds and set yourself free. Each person who embarks on this kind of healing journey helps to heal us all.

Catherine Cooper—Katie, as you like to be called—published and acclaimed author and editor, thank you for your expert mentorship with my writing and for your keen eye for challenging the structure and clarity of my messages. Without your guidance and encouragement, I am not sure I would have felt the confidence to write and publish my first book: *Open Me – the true story of a magical journey from fear to freedom.* Thank you from my whole heart.

Kaya Singer—artist, coach and business mentor—without your talented business mentorship and support I would have been like a canoe in an ocean storm with no paddle when I moved back to Canada. A million thank yous for helping to keep me steady and focused on what I said I wanted to create.

Sue Kerr—artist, gardener, writer and editor. Thank you for the editing work you do and the colour you bring to my writing. Just when I think I've almost finished something, you make me think about it from a different perspective, which is just what is needed. Thank you for the richness you bring.

About the author

I was born in Canada to a Scandinavian mother and a father of mixed heritage: English, French with rumours of Native American roots. My parents, being the more sensitive type as well as independent thinkers, each followed their own spiritual practices such as Transcendental Meditation and intuition practice.

As a child, I could see auras. I talked with the trees and the rocks. No one told me I was "making things up." In my early teens, I found an avenue to study and develop my intuition. I learned that psychic ability is innate for everyone. My passion for understanding the psyche led me to educate myself in various streams of psychology such as: Accelerated Learning, Transactional Analysis, ontological coaching, Neuro-Linguistic Programming, hypnotherapy, shamanism, and Multiple Brain Integration Techniques.

In 1993, I started a business designing and delivering courses and doing one-on-one coaching for organisations. I created a coaching methodology and trained and supervised coaches. As the business evolved, I offered courses on intuition development and ran shamanic weekend retreats. In my practice now, I work with clients through one-on-one sessions, public courses and retreats doing transformational work.

30 years ago, I met a New Zealander and moved to the southern hemisphere, where I lived for 29 years. Just over a year ago, following a strong inner calling, I sold

up everything in New Zealand and returned to Canada. For the first 12 months in North America, I lived in a truck camper touring with my first book from coast to coast doing talks and courses wherever I was. Canada is where I currently reside, guided by my *inner nudge*.

This is my second book. My first book was published in 2017 and is called, *Open Me – the true story of a magical journey from fear to freedom.* You can find out more about my work and current events on my website www.leannebabcock.com

Stay Connected

The work of a slayer-of-dragons is never done. If you are interested in staying tuned in to my journeys and other events and programs I host, you can:

Newsletter — https://leannebabcock.ca/leannes-newsletter/

Instagram — https://www.instagram.com/leannebabcock/

Facebook — https://www.facebook.com/leanne.babcock.spiritual.transformation.author

Website — https://leannebabcock.ca/

Blog — https://leannebabcock.ca/blog/

LinkedIn — https://www.linkedin.com/in/spiritualauthorleannebabcock/

COACHING PROGRAM

Maybe you're ready for my signature coaching program called: WOMAN (WO-MAN) BEAT YOUR DRUM. This program is for warriors-of-love, you, who want more in your life—much more. In this program, you will break free from old limiting thoughts that have held you back, to be the YOU that is truly, deeply in your heart. Are you ready? https://leannebabcock.ca/services/woman-beat-your-drum/

A GIFT FOR YOU

I refer to meditation on some of the pages of this book. Meditation, in one form or another, is the number one key in accessing your inner wisdom. Here is a 5-minute simple meditation that you can do at any time of the day to relax, slow down and be present. It was recorded in New Zealand with no music except the natural sounds of the breeze and the tapping wind chimes in the background.

You can collect your gift here:
https://leannebabcock.ca/5-minute-soothing-meditation/